The Ultimate Instagram Guide

From Beginner to Pro

Kiet Huynh

Table of Contents

Introduction

1.1 What Is Instagram and Why Use It?

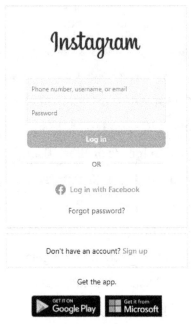

Introduction

Instagram is one of the most popular social media platforms in the world, with over a billion active users. Originally launched in 2010 as a photo-sharing app, it has evolved into a powerful platform for personal expression, business marketing, networking, and entertainment. Whether you are an individual looking to share your daily experiences, an influencer building a brand, or a business seeking to reach potential customers, Instagram provides a dynamic and engaging space to connect with the world.

This chapter will explore what Instagram is, its core functionalities, and the reasons why millions of people across the globe use it daily.

What Is Instagram?

Instagram is a social networking service that allows users to share photos and videos, interact with others, and discover content based on their interests. The platform is designed with a visually driven interface, emphasizing high-quality images, short videos, and engaging storytelling elements.

Instagram is available as a mobile app for both iOS and Android devices, with limited functionality accessible through a web browser. The platform has grown significantly since its inception, introducing features like Stories, Reels, IGTV, Shopping, and direct messaging, making it more than just a photo-sharing application.

Key Features of Instagram

1. **Posts:** Users can upload images and videos to their profiles, accompanied by captions, hashtags, and location tags.

2. **Stories:** Temporary posts that disappear after 24 hours, allowing users to share real-time updates with interactive features like polls, questions, and stickers.

3. **Reels:** Short-form videos (up to 90 seconds) with creative editing tools, audio overlays, and special effects.

4. **Explore Page:** A personalized feed that helps users discover new content, trending topics, and suggested accounts.

5. **Direct Messages (DMs):** A private messaging feature that allows users to communicate directly with individuals or groups.

6. **Shopping:** Businesses can showcase their products, link to e-commerce sites, and enable direct purchases within the app.

7. **Live Videos:** Users can broadcast in real-time to engage with followers interactively.

8. **IGTV (Instagram TV):** Long-form video content designed for creators and brands to share extended videos beyond the standard post limits.

These features provide a variety of ways for users to interact, express themselves, and connect with others.

Why Use Instagram?

There are many reasons why Instagram has become a dominant force in the social media landscape. Whether for personal, creative, or business purposes, Instagram offers unique advantages that make it an essential platform for millions of people.

1. Personal Expression and Creativity

Instagram is a great outlet for creativity. Users can edit and enhance their photos and videos with filters, effects, and captions, allowing them to express themselves uniquely. Many people use Instagram as a visual diary to document their experiences, travels, hobbies, and everyday moments.

2. Social Connection and Networking

Instagram bridges the gap between people, allowing users to connect with friends, family, celebrities, and influencers. Features like tagging, commenting, and direct messaging foster engagement and create a sense of community.

Additionally, Instagram is a valuable networking tool for professionals. Whether you're an artist, entrepreneur, or job seeker, Instagram provides opportunities to connect with like-minded individuals, industry experts, and potential clients.

3. Business and Brand Growth

For businesses and brands, Instagram is an invaluable marketing tool. The platform allows companies to:

- Showcase their products and services through high-quality visuals.
- Engage directly with customers through comments, messages, and interactive content.
- Run targeted ads to reach specific demographics and audiences.
- Utilize Instagram Shopping to drive sales directly from the platform.

Many businesses rely on Instagram to build brand awareness, establish credibility, and drive revenue.

4. Entertainment and Inspiration

Instagram is a hub of entertainment, featuring a constant stream of diverse content. Users can follow their favorite influencers, watch behind-the-scenes clips from celebrities, discover cooking recipes, get fashion inspiration, and much more.

Additionally, the Reels and Explore page introduce users to trending challenges, viral videos, and creative storytelling, making Instagram an engaging and enjoyable platform.

5. Learning and Education

Beyond entertainment, Instagram is also a source of valuable information. Many accounts specialize in educational content, providing tips on various topics, from fitness and mental health to finance and technology. Hashtags and community-driven content allow users to explore niche interests and stay informed about the latest trends.

6. Influence and Social Impact

Instagram is a powerful platform for raising awareness and advocating for social causes. Activists, organizations, and individuals use Instagram to spread messages about important issues, organize campaigns, and drive positive change.

From environmental movements to mental health awareness, Instagram enables users to engage with meaningful causes and inspire action.

Conclusion

Instagram is more than just a social media app—it is a platform that empowers users to share, connect, and grow. Whether you're using it for personal enjoyment, creative expression, business promotion, or networking, Instagram offers an array of tools to help you achieve your goals.

In the next chapters, we will explore how to set up an Instagram account, navigate its features, and optimize your experience for maximum engagement and success. Whether you're a complete beginner or looking to refine your skills, this guide will provide everything you need to master Instagram like a pro.

1.2 Who This Book Is For

Instagram has grown from a simple photo-sharing app into a powerful platform used by millions of individuals, influencers, businesses, and brands worldwide. Whether you want to connect with friends, showcase your creative work, grow a business, or establish a personal brand, Instagram offers endless possibilities. This book, *The Ultimate Instagram Guide: From Beginner to Pro*, is designed for anyone who wants to understand and master Instagram, regardless of experience level.

In this section, we will explore the different types of readers who will benefit from this book and how each group can use Instagram to achieve their goals.

1. Beginners Who Have Never Used Instagram Before

If you have never used Instagram before or have just created an account but feel lost, this book will guide you step by step. You may have questions such as:

- What is Instagram, and how does it work?

- How do I create an account and set up my profile?

- How can I find friends and start following people?

- What do terms like "Stories," "Reels," and "Hashtags" mean?

- How do I share my first post?

This book covers all these basic concepts and more. You will learn how to navigate Instagram's interface, interact with posts, and create engaging content. By following the instructions in this book, you will gain confidence in using Instagram and making the most of its features.

2. Casual Users Who Want to Enhance Their Instagram Experience

Many people already have an Instagram account but only use it occasionally. If you are someone who logs in once in a while, likes a few photos, and maybe posts a picture once every few months, this book will help you enhance your experience. You may be interested in:

- Learning how to create more engaging posts

- Discovering new features such as Reels and Instagram Stories

- Using Instagram as a way to connect with people who share similar interests

- Understanding how Instagram's algorithm works and how to see more relevant content

By the end of this book, casual users will have a better grasp of how to use Instagram more effectively, allowing them to engage with friends and content that matters to them.

3. Content Creators and Influencers Who Want to Grow Their Following

Are you a photographer, artist, writer, or musician looking to share your work with the world? Or do you dream of becoming an Instagram influencer with a large and engaged audience? Instagram is one of the best platforms for building a personal brand and reaching new audiences. However, growing a following on Instagram requires more than just posting pictures—it involves strategy, creativity, and consistency.

This book provides insights into:

- How to create high-quality and engaging content

- The best strategies for gaining followers organically

- How to use hashtags, geotags, and collaborations to expand your reach

- Tips for maintaining a strong presence on Instagram

For aspiring influencers, this book will also cover essential topics such as working with brands, monetizing content, and managing audience engagement.

4. Small Business Owners and Entrepreneurs

Instagram is an essential marketing tool for businesses of all sizes. Whether you run a local bakery, an online shop, or a global brand, Instagram provides a platform to showcase your products, engage with customers, and drive sales. If you are a business owner, this book will teach you how to:

- Set up a business profile and access Instagram analytics

- Create effective marketing campaigns

- Use Instagram Ads to reach a targeted audience

- Leverage Instagram Shopping to sell products directly on the platform

Instagram is not just about gaining followers; it's about building meaningful relationships with customers. By implementing the strategies in this book, businesses can increase brand awareness, boost customer engagement, and generate more revenue.

5. Social Media Managers and Marketers

If you are responsible for managing an Instagram account for a brand, company, or organization, this book will provide you with advanced insights on how to maximize engagement and grow an online community. Social media managers need to understand the latest Instagram trends, algorithms, and analytics. This book covers topics such as:

- How to craft a winning Instagram content strategy

- The importance of storytelling in social media marketing

- Best practices for running successful Instagram ad campaigns

- Measuring performance using Instagram Insights

By mastering these skills, social media managers can ensure that their brands remain relevant, competitive, and engaging in an ever-changing digital landscape.

6. Photographers, Videographers, and Creative Professionals

Instagram is a visual platform, making it an ideal space for creative professionals. Whether you are a photographer, videographer, graphic designer, or digital artist, Instagram can serve as both a portfolio and a networking tool. In this book, you will learn:

- How to showcase your work professionally on Instagram

- The best ways to edit and enhance your photos and videos for Instagram

- How to attract clients and collaborators through your Instagram presence

- Tips for using Instagram Stories, Reels, and IGTV to showcase your creative process

With Instagram, creative professionals have the opportunity to reach a global audience and connect with like-minded individuals, potential clients, and fellow artists.

7. Anyone Interested in Monetizing Instagram

Many people use Instagram as a source of income. Whether through brand partnerships, affiliate marketing, selling digital products, or promoting services, Instagram offers various monetization opportunities. This book will cover:

- The different ways to make money on Instagram

- How to qualify for Instagram's monetization programs

- The do's and don'ts of working with brands and sponsors

- How to maintain authenticity while promoting products

If you are looking to turn your Instagram presence into a side hustle or even a full-time career, this book will provide the strategies and knowledge you need.

8. Parents and Educators Who Want to Understand Instagram

Many parents and educators want to understand how Instagram works so they can guide young users safely. If you are a parent concerned about your child's online activities, this book will help you:

- Understand Instagram's privacy and security settings

- Learn how to set up parental controls and manage screen time

- Teach young users about online safety and responsible social media use

Educators can also use Instagram as a tool for engagement, whether by sharing educational content or connecting with students in meaningful ways.

Final Thoughts

No matter your background or goals, this book is designed to help you become more confident and successful on Instagram. Whether you are a beginner just starting out or an experienced user looking to refine your strategy, *The Ultimate Instagram Guide: From Beginner to Pro* provides the knowledge and tools you need to thrive on the platform.

As you progress through this book, keep in mind that Instagram is constantly evolving, with new features and trends emerging regularly. The key to success is staying adaptable, experimenting with new content, and always engaging with your audience in meaningful ways.

Now that you know who this book is for, let's dive into the world of Instagram and start your journey toward becoming an expert user!

1.3 How to Use This Guide

Explore What's New

Our continuously evolving features empower you to express yourself in new ways.

Features →

Welcome to **The Ultimate Instagram Guide: From Beginner to Pro**! Whether you are new to Instagram or looking to refine your skills, this book is designed to help you navigate the platform effectively. To make the most of this guide, it is essential to understand how the content is structured and how you can apply the information to your Instagram journey. This section will provide an overview of how to use this book efficiently, ensuring you gain the most valuable insights with minimal confusion.

Understanding the Structure of This Guide

This guide is organized into several chapters, each covering a specific aspect of Instagram. The chapters are structured to gradually build your knowledge, starting with the basics and moving on to more advanced strategies. Here's how the book is laid out:

- **Introduction**: Explains what Instagram is, why you should use it, and who this book is intended for.

- **Chapter 1: Getting Started with Instagram**: Covers account creation, profile setup, and the basic navigation of the app.

- **Chapter 2: Posting and Engaging on Instagram**: Guides you through content creation, using stories and reels, and interacting with other users.

- **Chapter 3: Growing Your Audience**: Teaches you how to increase your followers, optimize engagement, and leverage Instagram's algorithm.

- **Chapter 4: Advanced Instagram Strategies**: Focuses on branding, collaborations, and using Instagram for business purposes.

- **Chapter 5: Analytics and Optimization**: Helps you understand Instagram Insights and refine your content strategy based on data.

- **Chapter 6: Monetizing Instagram**: Explores different ways to earn money through Instagram, including partnerships and product sales.

- **Chapter 7: Staying Safe and Managing Your Account**: Provides tips on account security, handling negativity, and managing multiple accounts.

- **Conclusion**: Summarizes key takeaways and next steps for continued success on Instagram.

Each chapter is divided into smaller sections, making it easy to find the information you need without having to read the entire book at once.

How to Navigate This Guide

Read in Order or Jump to Specific Sections

This book is designed to be read in a linear progression for beginners, as each chapter builds upon the previous one. However, if you are already familiar with Instagram and looking for specific information, you can skip ahead to the relevant chapters without missing essential concepts.

For example:

- If you are a complete beginner, start with **Chapter 1: Getting Started with Instagram** and follow through sequentially.

- If you already have an account but want to improve engagement, go directly to **Chapter 3: Growing Your Audience**.

- If you are a business owner looking to monetize, jump to **Chapter 6: Monetizing Instagram**.

Apply What You Learn

Instagram is a practical, hands-on platform, so the best way to learn is by doing. As you go through this book, try to apply the techniques and strategies immediately to see what works best for your specific needs. The book includes:

- **Step-by-step instructions**: Follow these guides to set up and optimize your Instagram account.

- **Actionable tips**: Use practical tips provided in each chapter to enhance your Instagram experience.

- **Case studies and examples**: Learn from real-world examples of successful Instagram users.

- **Exercises and challenges**: At the end of some sections, you'll find exercises to reinforce what you've learned.

Use the Book as a Reference

Even after reading the book, you may want to revisit certain sections as you gain experience on Instagram. To make this easier:

- Each chapter has clear **subheadings** so you can quickly locate relevant information.

- Key points are **highlighted** to make them easy to remember.

- The **index at the back** of the book helps you find topics quickly.

Who Can Benefit from This Guide?

This book is written for a diverse audience, including:

- **Complete beginners** who have never used Instagram before.

- **Casual users** who want to improve their presence and engagement.

- **Influencers and content creators** looking to build their personal brand.

- **Business owners** who want to leverage Instagram for marketing and sales.

- **Marketers and social media managers** seeking advanced strategies for professional growth.

Regardless of your level of experience, you will find valuable insights tailored to your needs.

Additional Resources

To enhance your learning experience, this book provides additional resources:

- **Helpful tools**: Recommended third-party apps for editing, scheduling, and analytics.

- **Online communities**: Links to forums, groups, and networks where you can connect with other Instagram users.

- **Updates and changes**: Since social media platforms evolve, visit the provided website link for updates on Instagram's latest features.

Final Tips Before You Begin

1. **Keep an Open Mind** – Instagram is constantly evolving, so be prepared to experiment with new features and trends.

2. **Be Consistent** – Building an Instagram presence takes time; consistency is key to success.

3. **Engage with Others** – Instagram is a social platform, and engagement is just as important as content creation.

4. **Track Your Progress** – Regularly check Instagram Insights to see what works and adjust accordingly.

By following this guide, you will gain the confidence and knowledge to use Instagram effectively, whether for personal enjoyment, brand building, or business success. Now, let's get started!

CHAPTER I
Getting Started with Instagram

2.1 Creating an Instagram Account

2.1.1 Downloading and Installing the App

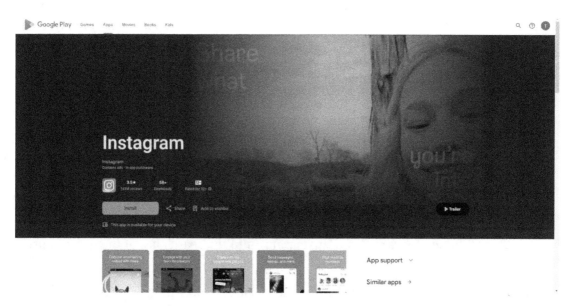

Introduction

Instagram is a widely used social media platform available on multiple devices, including smartphones, tablets, and desktops. However, the most common way to use Instagram is through its mobile app. This section provides a detailed, step-by-step guide on downloading and installing the Instagram app on different devices, ensuring that users can easily set up and begin their Instagram journey.

Downloading Instagram on Mobile Devices

Instagram is available for download on both iOS and Android devices through their respective app stores: the Apple App Store and Google Play Store. Below are the steps for each platform.

Downloading Instagram on iOS (iPhone and iPad)

1. **Open the App Store**: Locate the App Store icon on your iPhone or iPad and tap to open it.

2. **Search for Instagram**: In the search bar at the bottom of the screen, type "Instagram" and press the search button.

3. **Select the Official Instagram App**: Look for the app with the Instagram logo (a colorful camera icon) and verify that it is developed by "Instagram, Inc."

4. **Tap the Download Button**: Click on the download button (cloud icon with an arrow or "Get" button). If prompted, authenticate with your Apple ID, Face ID, or Touch ID.

5. **Wait for the Installation to Complete**: The app will begin downloading, and once finished, it will automatically install on your device.

6. **Open Instagram**: Tap the Instagram icon on your home screen to launch the app.

Downloading Instagram on Android

1. **Open Google Play Store**: Locate the Google Play Store app on your Android device and tap to open it.

2. **Search for Instagram**: Type "Instagram" into the search bar at the top and press enter.

3. **Select the Official Instagram App**: Look for the app with the Instagram logo and confirm it is developed by "Instagram, Inc."

4. **Tap the Install Button**: Press the green "Install" button to begin downloading the app.

5. **Wait for the Installation to Complete**: The app will be installed automatically after downloading.

6. **Open Instagram**: Tap the Instagram icon in your app drawer or home screen to launch the app.

Installing Instagram on Desktop (Windows & macOS)

While Instagram is primarily designed for mobile devices, you can still use it on a desktop by accessing its web version or downloading the app on Windows.

Using Instagram on a Web Browser

1. **Open Your Preferred Web Browser**: Instagram works well on Chrome, Safari, Firefox, and Edge.

2. **Go to the Official Website**: Type https://www.instagram.com/ in the address bar and press enter.

3. **Sign In or Sign Up**: If you already have an account, enter your login details. Otherwise, proceed with signing up.

4. **Explore Instagram**: While the web version has limited features compared to the mobile app, you can still browse posts, like content, and send messages.

Downloading Instagram on Windows

1. **Open Microsoft Store**: Click on the Start menu and search for "Microsoft Store."\2. **Search for Instagram**: Type "Instagram" in the search bar and find the official app.

2. **Download and Install**: Click the "Install" button and wait for the process to complete.

3. **Launch Instagram**: Open the app and log in to start using Instagram on your PC.

Troubleshooting Common Installation Issues

1. Insufficient Storage Space

If your device does not have enough storage, you may encounter installation errors. To resolve this:

• Delete unnecessary apps or media files to free up space.

- Check your device's storage under settings and ensure at least 200MB is available for Instagram.

2. App Not Available in Store

Some users might not find Instagram in their app store due to regional restrictions. Solutions include:

- Checking if your device's location settings are correct.

- Using a VPN if Instagram is blocked in your country.

- Updating your app store settings to match the correct region.

3. Slow Download Speeds

If the app is downloading slowly, try the following:

- Ensure your device is connected to a stable Wi-Fi network.

- Restart your device and try again.

- Clear your app store cache (on Android) to refresh downloads.

Conclusion

Downloading and installing Instagram is a straightforward process across various platforms. By following the steps outlined in this guide, users can ensure they have the latest version of Instagram installed and ready to use. The next section will cover setting up your profile, helping you personalize your Instagram experience from the start.

2.1.2 Setting Up Your Profile

Introduction

Setting up your Instagram profile is one of the most crucial steps in establishing your presence on the platform. Whether you're using Instagram for personal use, content creation, or business purposes, a well-optimized profile makes a strong first impression and helps others understand who you are and what you offer. In this section, we will guide you through the essential elements of setting up a compelling Instagram profile, from choosing the right profile picture to writing an engaging bio and adding important links.

Choosing the Right Profile Picture

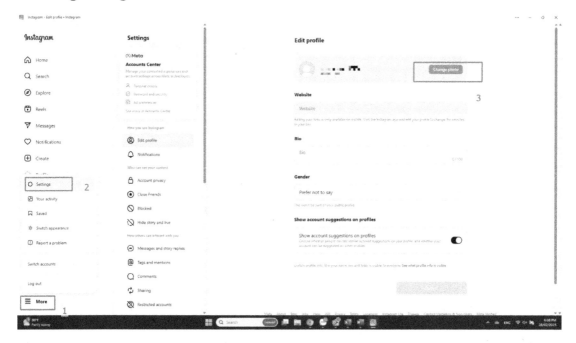

Your profile picture is the first visual element people notice when they visit your profile or see your comments and likes on other posts. Here are some key points to consider when selecting your profile picture:

1. Use a High-Quality Image

- Ensure the image is clear, high-resolution, and well-lit.

- Avoid blurry or pixelated photos, as they can make your profile appear unprofessional.

2. Keep It Simple and Recognizable

- If you're an individual, use a close-up of your face with a neutral or simple background.

- If you're a brand or business, consider using your logo or a branded icon.

- Make sure the image is easily recognizable even when displayed as a small thumbnail.

3. Ensure It's Centered and Properly Cropped

- Instagram displays profile pictures in a circular frame, so ensure your subject is centered.

- Use a tool like Canva or Photoshop to crop your image correctly.

Writing an Engaging Bio

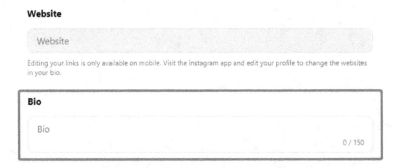

Your Instagram bio is a short but powerful description that tells people who you are and what you do. It appears under your username on your profile page.

1. Keep It Concise and Informative

- Instagram bios have a 150-character limit, so make every word count.

- Highlight the most important aspects of your personal brand, business, or interests.

2. Use Keywords and Emojis Wisely

- Keywords help people understand what you do at a glance.

- Emojis can make your bio visually appealing and break up text, but don't overuse them.

3. Include a Call-to-Action (CTA)

- Direct your audience to take an action, such as visiting your website, checking out your latest post, or following a hashtag.

- Examples:

    o "✉ DM for collaborations!"

- o   "🚀 New blog post! Click the link below."

4. Add Your Contact Information (For Business Accounts)

- If you have a business account, Instagram allows you to add a contact button.

- Include an email address or phone number to make it easy for people to reach you.

Adding Links and Contact Information

Instagram provides limited options for linking to external sites, but you can still make the most of it.

1. Using the Website Field

- You can add one clickable link in your bio, so choose wisely.

- Options include:

  - o   Your personal website

  - o   A link aggregator like Linktree or Beacons

  - o   A specific product or blog post

2. Utilizing Instagram's Business Features

- Business and creator accounts can add additional contact buttons such as "Email" and "Call."

- These features make it easier for customers or followers to reach you directly.

3. Leveraging Story Highlights

- Use Story Highlights to provide permanent access to important links, promotions, or introductions.

Enabling Profile Privacy and Security Settings

Instagram allows users to customize their privacy settings based on their needs.

1. Public vs. Private Accounts

- **Public Profile:** Recommended for influencers, businesses, and brands to maximize reach.

- **Private Profile:** Best for personal users who want to limit access to their posts.

2. Two-Factor Authentication (2FA)

- Enable 2FA for additional security by linking your account to an authentication app or your phone number.

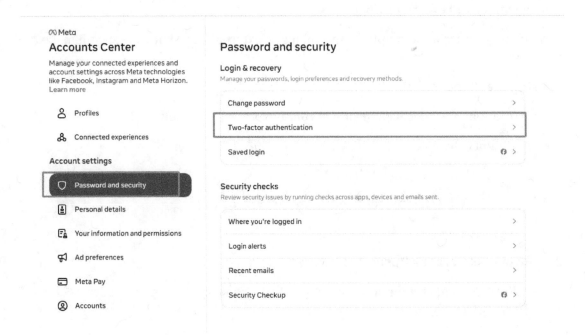

3. Managing Account Visibility

- Choose whether your activity status is visible to others.

- Restrict unwanted interactions by using Instagram's block and restrict features.

Optimizing Your Username and Handle

Your Instagram handle (@username) is your unique identifier on the platform. It should be easy to remember and relevant to your brand or personal identity.

1. Choosing an Effective Username

- Keep it short and simple.

- Avoid excessive numbers or special characters.

- Use your real name or business name for brand consistency.

2. Updating Your Display Name

- Your display name appears in your bio and is searchable.

- Use a name that complements your handle, such as including your niche or profession.

Finalizing Your Profile Setup

Once you've completed these steps, review your profile as a visitor to see if it's clear, engaging, and visually appealing. Ensure all information is accurate and up-to-date. Congratulations, you're now ready to start engaging with the Instagram community!

Summary

Setting up your Instagram profile properly is essential for building a strong presence on the platform. By selecting the right profile picture, writing a compelling bio, adding useful links, and optimizing privacy settings, you create a profile that attracts and retains followers. Now that your profile is complete, it's time to start exploring Instagram and creating content!

2.1.3 Understanding Account Types (Personal, Creator, Business)

Instagram offers three main types of accounts: Personal, Creator, and Business. Each type serves different purposes and provides unique features tailored to specific users. Choosing the right account type is crucial as it affects your access to analytics, monetization, and engagement tools. In this section, we will explore the differences between these account types, their key features, and how to select the best one for your needs.

1. Personal Account

A Personal account is the default option when signing up for Instagram. It is designed for individuals who use Instagram for casual purposes, such as sharing personal moments, engaging with friends and family, and following their favorite accounts.

Key Features of a Personal Account

- **Private or Public Profile:** Users can choose to keep their profile private, allowing only approved followers to see their posts, or set it to public for anyone to view.

- **Access to Basic Instagram Features:** This includes posting photos, videos, Stories, Reels, IGTV, and interacting with others via likes, comments, and direct messages.

- **No Advanced Analytics:** Personal accounts do not have access to Instagram Insights, which provides detailed data on audience engagement and performance.

- **Limited Monetization Options:** Unlike Creator and Business accounts, Personal accounts do not have access to Instagram's monetization features, such as branded content tools and Instagram Shopping.

Who Should Use a Personal Account?

- Individuals who use Instagram purely for social interaction and personal sharing.

- Users who prefer to keep their content private.

- Those who do not require analytics or promotional tools.

2. Creator Account

The Creator account is designed for influencers, content creators, public figures, and individuals who want more control over their audience engagement. It provides advanced insights, flexible messaging options, and monetization tools.

Key Features of a Creator Account

- **Access to Instagram Insights:** Provides detailed analytics about followers, engagement, reach, and content performance.

- **Category Labeling:** Users can choose from various categories (e.g., Blogger, Musician, Public Figure) to help define their profile.

- **Flexible Messaging Tools:** Messages are divided into three tabs: Primary, General, and Requests, allowing users to manage interactions more efficiently.

- **Branded Content Tools:** Enables collaboration with brands through sponsored posts and partnerships.

- **Monetization Features:** Includes IGTV ads, badges during Instagram Live, and Instagram Shopping for eligible users.

- **Music Library Access:** Unlike Business accounts, Creator accounts have full access to Instagram's licensed music library for use in Reels and Stories.

Who Should Use a Creator Account?

- Influencers and digital creators looking to grow their audience.

- Public figures who want to interact effectively with fans.

- Users who collaborate with brands for sponsorships and partnerships.

- Content creators who need detailed analytics and monetization tools.

3. Business Account

The Business account is designed for companies, brands, and entrepreneurs who use Instagram for marketing, customer engagement, and sales. It offers extensive tools for advertising, analytics, and customer communication.

Key Features of a Business Account

- **Instagram Insights:** Provides comprehensive data on follower demographics, engagement, and post performance.

- **Instagram Ads and Promotions:** Allows businesses to create paid advertisements and boost posts to reach a wider audience.

- **Contact Buttons:** Enables direct communication via phone, email, or directions linked to a physical location.

- **Instagram Shopping:** Businesses can set up an online storefront, tag products in posts, and enable in-app purchases.

- **Automated Messaging:** Provides quick replies and saved responses for customer inquiries.

- **Category Selection:** Businesses can label their profile with industry-specific categories (e.g., Retail, Health & Beauty, Food & Beverage).

Who Should Use a Business Account?

- Companies and brands looking to promote products and services.

- Entrepreneurs who sell directly through Instagram.

- Marketers and social media managers handling corporate accounts.

- Businesses that rely on advertising and customer engagement for growth.

4. Switching Between Account Types

Instagram allows users to switch between Personal, Creator, and Business accounts at any time. However, switching may impact certain features. For example:

- Moving from **Personal to Creator or Business** enables access to analytics and promotional tools.

- Switching from **Creator or Business to Personal** removes access to Instagram Insights and monetization features.

- Transitioning from **Business to Creator** restores access to the full Instagram music library.

How to Switch Account Types

1. Open the **Instagram app** and go to your **Profile**.

2. Tap the **Menu** (≡) in the top-right corner and select **Settings and Privacy**.

Account type and tools

Account type

Switch to professional account   >

3. Scroll down and tap **Account Type and Tools**.

4. Select **Switch to Personal Account**, **Switch to Creator Account**, or **Switch to Business Account**.

5. Follow the on-screen instructions to complete the transition.

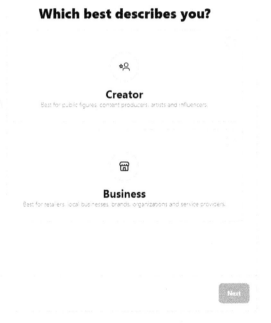

Which best describes you?

Creator

Best for public figures, content producers, artists and influencers.

Business

Best for retailers, local businesses, brands, organizations and service providers.

Next

5. Choosing the Right Account Type

When deciding on the best account type, consider your goals:

- If you use Instagram casually and prioritize privacy, **Personal** is the best option.

- If you are an influencer or content creator looking to grow and monetize, **Creator** is ideal.

- If you own a business or sell products/services, **Business** is the most suitable choice.

Conclusion

Understanding Instagram's different account types is essential for maximizing your experience on the platform. Whether you are a casual user, an aspiring influencer, or a business owner, selecting the right account type ensures you get the most out of Instagram's features. By making an informed decision, you can optimize your engagement, expand your reach, and achieve your social media goals.

2.2 Navigating the Instagram Interface

2.2.1 Home Feed and Posts

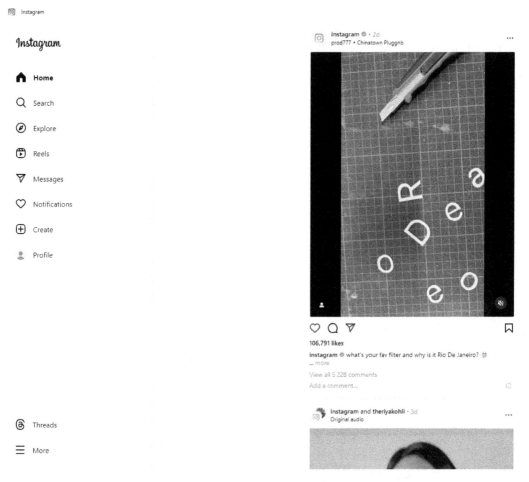

Instagram's **Home Feed** is the central hub where users interact with content from the accounts they follow. It is designed to provide a seamless experience for browsing, engaging with posts, and staying updated with the latest activities of friends, influencers, and brands. Understanding how the Home Feed works is crucial for anyone looking to make the most out of Instagram, whether as a casual user, content creator, or business.

Understanding the Home Feed

When you open Instagram, the Home Feed is the first screen you see. It consists of:

- **Posts from accounts you follow** – These can be photos, videos, carousels, or Reels shared by users you have chosen to follow.

- **Sponsored posts and advertisements** – Instagram integrates ads into your feed based on your interests and browsing history.

- **Suggested content** – Instagram may recommend posts from accounts you do not follow, but that align with your interactions and interests.

- **Stories bar at the top** – Quick-access circles at the top of the screen showing recently updated Stories from your followed accounts.

- **Navigation icons** – At the bottom of the feed, you will find navigation icons for Home, Search (Explore), Reels, Shopping, and your Profile.

The Home Feed is customized using Instagram's algorithm, which determines which posts appear first based on user engagement, relationships, and relevance.

How Posts Appear in the Home Feed

The Instagram algorithm prioritizes content based on various factors, including:

- **Engagement:** Posts with more likes, comments, and shares are more likely to appear higher in the feed.

- **Recency:** Newer posts generally appear first unless an older post has significant engagement.

- **User interactions:** Instagram tracks your interactions (likes, comments, shares, saves) and prioritizes similar content.

- **Time spent on posts:** The longer you view a post, the more likely Instagram will show similar content in the future.

Navigating and Interacting with Posts

1. Viewing Posts

Users can scroll through their Home Feed to browse content. Posts appear in chronological order based on Instagram's ranking system.

Each post typically includes:

- **Username and profile picture** – Clicking on the username takes you to the poster's profile.

- **Image or video content** – The main media of the post.

- **Caption** – The description or message from the user.

- **Engagement buttons** – Like, comment, share, and save options.

- **Post timestamp** – Showing when the post was published.

- **Location tag (optional)** – If the user has tagged a location, it appears under their username.

2. Engaging with Posts

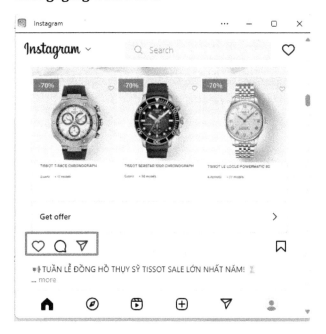

Instagram is a social platform, and interacting with posts is key to staying connected with your community. Ways to engage include:

Liking a Post

- Tap the **heart icon** below a post to like it.

- Double-tap the image or video to like it.

- Liked posts turn red, indicating your interaction.

Commenting on a Post

- Tap the **speech bubble icon** to open the comments section.
- Type your comment and hit **Post**.
- Tag users by typing **@username** in the comment.

Sharing a Post

- Tap the **paper plane icon** to send a post to friends via Direct Messages (DMs).
- Select "Add post to your story" to share it as a Story.

Saving a Post

- Tap the **bookmark icon** to save a post.
- Saved posts are stored in the "Saved" section of your profile for later viewing.

3. Posting to Your Home Feed

If you want to share content, Instagram allows different types of posts:

Creating a Photo Post

1. Tap the **+ icon** at the top or bottom of the Home Feed.

2. Select an image from your gallery or take a new photo.

3. Edit using Instagram filters and tools.

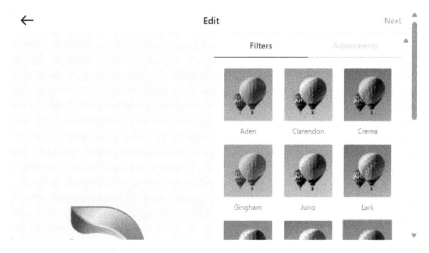

4. Add a caption, hashtags, and tag people.

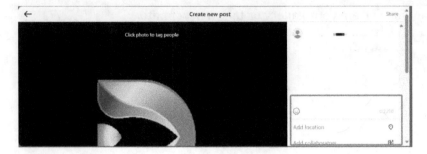

5. Tap **Share** to post.

Creating a Video Post

- Follow the same steps as a photo post, but select a video.

- Videos can be up to **60 seconds long** for standard posts.

Creating a Carousel Post

- Select multiple photos or videos (up to 10).

- Swipe through to arrange the order.

- Edit each media individually before posting.

Customizing Your Feed Experience

Instagram allows users to personalize their feed by:

- **Muting accounts** – You can mute posts from specific accounts without unfollowing them.

- **Hiding posts** – If you don't want to see a particular post, tap the three-dot menu and select "Not Interested."

- **Following new accounts** – To expand your feed, follow more users that align with your interests.

- **Interacting with specific content** – Engaging more with preferred content helps Instagram curate your feed accordingly.

Tips for a Better Home Feed Experience

- **Follow accounts that inspire you** – Whether it's for entertainment, business, or hobbies, curate your feed based on your preferences.

- **Engage regularly** – The more you interact, the more relevant your feed will be.

- **Utilize the "Following" and "Favorites" filters** – Instagram allows you to view posts only from people you follow or from a hand-picked favorite list.

- **Limit distractions** – If Instagram feels overwhelming, use the "Take a Break" feature to set reminders for usage time limits.

Conclusion

The **Home Feed** is a dynamic and personalized space that keeps you connected with people and content that matter most. By understanding how posts appear and how to engage effectively, you can make Instagram a more enjoyable and purposeful experience. Whether you're here to share moments, grow a brand, or stay updated, mastering the Home Feed is the first step in leveraging Instagram to its fullest potential.

2.2.2 Stories and Reels Section

Instagram's **Stories and Reels** sections are two of the most dynamic and engaging features on the platform. These tools allow users to share short-lived content (Stories) and highly engaging short videos (Reels) that enhance interaction, visibility, and creativity. Understanding how to navigate, create, and optimize content in these sections is crucial for both casual users and businesses.

Understanding Instagram Stories

What Are Instagram Stories?

Instagram Stories are temporary posts that disappear after 24 hours unless saved as **Highlights**. They appear at the top of the Instagram home screen and allow users to share images, videos, text, and interactive elements like polls and stickers.

Navigating the Stories Section

To access Stories, tap on **your profile picture** or the profile pictures of other users at the top of your home feed. Here's how you can navigate through them:

- **Tap** to move to the next Story.

- **Swipe left** to jump to the next user's Stories.

- **Swipe right** to return to the previous user's Stories.

- **Press and hold** to pause a Story for a closer look.

- **Swipe down** to exit Stories.

Creating an Instagram Story

To create a Story, follow these steps:

1. Tap on **Your Story** at the top-left of the home screen or swipe right from anywhere in the feed.

2. Capture a new photo/video or upload one from your gallery.

3. Edit using various Instagram features:

   o **Text:** Add captions, quotes, or messages.

   o **Stickers:** Use GIFs, location tags, polls, questions, and emojis.

   o **Filters:** Swipe left/right for different effects.

   o **Draw:** Use the pen tool to highlight parts of the image/video.

   o **Music:** Add background music from Instagram's library.

4. Tap **Send To** and choose **Your Story** or select specific followers.

5. Tap **Share** to publish.

Using Instagram Story Highlights

Highlights allow you to save your best Stories permanently on your profile. To create a Highlight:

1. Go to your profile and tap **New (+)** under the Highlights section.

2. Select past Stories you want to include.

3. Choose a cover and name your Highlight.

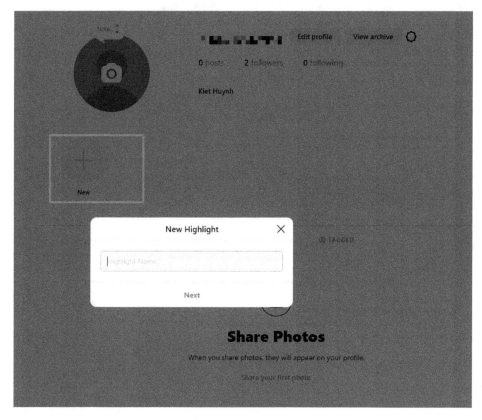

4. Tap **Add** to save.

Interacting with Instagram Stories

- **Reply to Stories:** Swipe up and send a message.

- **React with emojis:** Tap the emoji reaction bar.

- **Share a Story:** Tap the paper airplane icon to forward.

- **Mute/unmute Stories:** Long press a user's Story and select **Mute/Unmute**.

Understanding Instagram Reels

What Are Instagram Reels?

Reels are short-form, multi-clip videos that can be up to **90 seconds long**. They include effects, text, audio, and interactive features, making them highly engaging.

Navigating the Reels Section

To find Reels:

- **Explore Page:** Reels appear in the discovery tab (magnifying glass icon).

- **Dedicated Reels Tab:** On a user's profile, look for the Reels icon.

- **Scrolling Feed:** Instagram suggests Reels based on interests.

Creating an Instagram Reel

To create a Reel:

1. Open Instagram and swipe right or tap the **+** icon, then select **Reel**.

2. Record a video or upload clips.

3. Edit using built-in tools:

   o **Audio:** Add trending sounds or voiceovers.

   o **Effects:** Use AR filters, transitions, and speed controls.

   o **Text and Stickers:** Include captions and interactive elements.

   o **Align Feature:** Ensures smooth transitions between clips.

4. Tap **Next**, write a caption, select hashtags, and adjust sharing settings.

5. Choose whether to post on **Reels only** or also in your **Feed**.

6. Tap **Share** to publish.

Optimizing Reels for Engagement

- **Use Trending Audio:** Boosts visibility in the algorithm.

- **Engaging Captions:** Encourage comments and shares.

- **High-Quality Video:** Clear visuals and good lighting matter.

- **Hashtags & Tags:** Use relevant tags to reach a wider audience.

- **Call-to-Action (CTA):** Ask viewers to like, comment, or follow.

Conclusion

Instagram's Stories and Reels sections provide powerful tools for sharing content in a fun, engaging way. By mastering these features, users can enhance their presence on the platform, whether for personal use, branding, or business growth. Understanding how to navigate, create, and optimize Stories and Reels will significantly improve your Instagram experience.

2.2.3 Explore Page and Search Function

Introduction to the Explore Page

Instagram's **Explore Page** is a powerful feature designed to help users discover new content tailored to their interests. It provides a curated selection of posts, reels, and stories from accounts that users may not follow but might find interesting. The Explore Page is personalized for each user based on their activity, engagement, and preferences, making it an essential tool for content discovery and networking.

In this section, we will explore the various elements of the Explore Page, how the Instagram algorithm determines what appears there, and how users can utilize the search function to find specific content, hashtags, and accounts.

Understanding the Layout of the Explore Page

When you navigate to the Explore Page by tapping the **magnifying glass icon** at the bottom of your Instagram app, you will see a dynamic feed of content. The layout typically includes:

1. **Top Posts** – Popular and trending posts based on Instagram's algorithm.

2. **Reels Section** – A curated selection of short videos aligned with user interests.

3. **Stories Highlights** – Featured Instagram Stories from public accounts or influencers.

4. **Category-Based Suggestions** – Topics like travel, fashion, fitness, and food that users can explore further.

5. **IGTV and Video Recommendations** – Longer-form content suggestions tailored to user preferences.

6. **Shopping Section** – A personalized collection of product recommendations from Instagram Shops.

Each time a user visits the Explore Page, it refreshes with new content based on recent activity. This means the page is never static and constantly evolves to match user behavior.

How the Instagram Algorithm Personalizes Your Explore Page

Instagram's Explore Page is powered by a complex algorithm that determines what appears on an individual's feed. The key factors influencing the content shown include:

- **User Interaction** – Posts, accounts, and hashtags you engage with frequently.

- **Content Similarity** – Posts similar to the ones you have liked or saved.

- **Popularity of Posts** – Trending posts with high engagement may appear in Explore.

- **Location-Based Recommendations** – Content from nearby users or places.

- **Account and Interest Signals** – Instagram analyzes your behavior to predict content you may like.

The more you interact with certain types of content, the more refined and personalized your Explore Page becomes over time.

The Search Function: Finding Content, Accounts, and Hashtags

The **Search Function** on Instagram is a powerful tool that allows users to find specific content, accounts, hashtags, locations, and even trending topics.

Accessing the Search Feature

To use the search function:

1. Tap the **magnifying glass icon** at the bottom of the app to access the Explore Page.

2. Tap the **search bar** at the top of the screen.

3. Enter a keyword, hashtag, username, or location to start searching.

4. Browse through the relevant results displayed under different categories.

Types of Searches

Instagram's search feature is divided into several categories:

1. **Top Searches** – The most relevant results based on your search term.

2. **Accounts** – Profiles that match your query.

3. **Tags (Hashtags)** – Popular hashtags related to your search term.

4. **Places (Locations)** – Geotagged posts and places near or related to your search.

5. **Audio** – Trending audio tracks used in Reels and Stories.

Using these categories, users can refine their search and discover new content in a more organized way.

Optimizing Your Content for the Explore Page and Search Function

For content creators, appearing on the Explore Page can lead to massive engagement and increased followers. Here are some strategies to optimize your posts:

1. Use Relevant Hashtags

Hashtags play a crucial role in discoverability. Using **popular, relevant, and niche-specific hashtags** can help your content appear in search results and the Explore Page.

2. Engage Consistently

Interacting with followers, responding to comments, and engaging with similar accounts can improve your chances of getting featured on Explore.

3. Post High-Quality Content

Instagram prioritizes visually appealing and engaging content. High-resolution images, well-edited videos, and creative captions improve your content's visibility.

4. Utilize Reels and IGTV

Video content, especially Reels, is favored by Instagram's algorithm. Regularly posting Reels can increase your chances of appearing on the Explore Page.

5. Optimize Your Profile and Bio

A well-crafted Instagram bio with relevant keywords and links enhances your discoverability in search results.

Conclusion

The Explore Page and Search Function are powerful tools that enhance content discovery on Instagram. Whether you are a casual user looking for inspiration or a content creator aiming to expand your reach, understanding how these features work will help you navigate Instagram more effectively. By engaging with content strategically and optimizing your posts, you can make the most out of Instagram's algorithm to grow your presence and find valuable content aligned with your interests.

2.2.4 Profile Page and Settings

Edit profile

Change photo

Website

Website

Editing your links is only available on mobile. Visit the Instagram app and edit your profile to change the websites in your bio.

Bio

Bio

0 / 150

Gender

Male

This won't be part of your public profile.

Show account suggestions on profiles

Show account suggestions on profiles
Choose whether people can see similar account suggestions on your profile, and whether your account can be suggested on other profiles.

Certain profile info, like your name, bio and links, is visible to everyone. See what profile info is visible

Your Instagram profile page is your personal or brand identity on the platform. It is where visitors can learn about you, see your posts, and interact with your content. In this section, we will explore the different elements of the profile page, how to customize it, and how to optimize the settings to enhance your Instagram experience.

Understanding the Profile Page Layout

When you navigate to your profile page, you will see several key elements:

1. Profile Picture

Your profile picture is the first visual element users see when they visit your profile. It also appears next to your username across Instagram, such as in comments and direct messages. Choose a clear, high-quality image that represents you or your brand. For businesses and influencers, using a recognizable logo or headshot is recommended.

2. Username and Name

- **Username (@handle):** Your unique identifier on Instagram. It should be easy to remember and relevant to your personal brand or business.

- **Name:** This is a separate field from your username and can be a full name, business name, or a keyword to help with discoverability.

3. Bio

Your bio is a short description that appears under your name. It is limited to 150 characters, so make it concise and engaging. A great bio typically includes:

- Who you are or what you do

- A call to action (e.g., "DM me for collaborations!" or "Follow for daily tips!")

- Emojis to make it visually appealing

- Hashtags or mentions if relevant

4. Website Link

Instagram allows you to add one clickable link in your bio. You can use it to direct followers to your website, portfolio, blog, or a link aggregator like Linktree to display multiple links.

5. Contact Buttons (For Business and Creator Accounts)

If you have a business or creator account, you can enable contact buttons such as "Email," "Call," or "Directions," making it easy for followers to connect with you.

6. Story Highlights

Story Highlights allow you to keep selected Stories on your profile beyond the standard 24-hour limit. They appear as circular icons under your bio. You can categorize them into different topics such as "Products," "Testimonials," or "Behind the Scenes."

7. Posts Grid

Your posts are displayed in a grid format. The layout is crucial for maintaining a cohesive aesthetic. Many brands and influencers use specific color schemes or themes to make their profile visually appealing.

8. Followers and Following Count

These numbers show how many people follow you and how many accounts you follow. While high follower counts can indicate popularity, engagement is a more important metric.

Customizing Your Profile Settings

Your profile settings allow you to control privacy, notifications, security, and account preferences. Here's how to access and adjust them:

1. Accessing Settings

1.   Go to your **Profile Page** by tapping your profile picture at the bottom right.

2.   Tap the **Menu (☰) button** at the top right corner.

3.   Select **Settings and Privacy** from the dropdown menu.

2. Privacy Settings

Instagram offers various privacy options to control who can interact with your content:

- **Private Account:** Only approved followers can see your posts and stories.

- **Blocked Accounts:** Prevent specific users from viewing your content or contacting you.

- **Restricted Accounts:** Limits interactions from certain users without blocking them entirely.

- **Hidden Words:** Automatically filters offensive comments and messages.

- **Activity Status:** Choose whether to show when you were last active.

3. Security Settings

To keep your account secure, explore the following options:

- **Two-Factor Authentication (2FA):** Adds an extra layer of security by requiring a code when logging in from a new device.

- **Login Activity:** Displays recent login locations and devices used to access your account.

- **Saved Login Info:** Decide whether Instagram should remember your login credentials.

4. Notification Preferences

Manage which types of notifications you receive:

- **Push Notifications:** Control alerts for likes, comments, follows, messages, and more.

- **Email and SMS Notifications:** Receive updates about Instagram activity via email or text.

- **Live and Video Notifications:** Customize alerts for live streams, IGTV, and Reels.

5. Account Preferences

Adjust your Instagram experience to match your preferences:

- **Switching Account Type:** Convert between Personal, Creator, and Business accounts.

- **Linked Accounts:** Connect Instagram to Facebook, Twitter, or other platforms.

- **Language Settings:** Change the language of the app.

- **Data Usage:** Manage mobile data consumption when using Instagram.

Optimizing Your Profile for Growth

A well-optimized profile can help attract more followers and increase engagement. Here are some tips:

1. Choose a Memorable Username and Bio

- Keep your username short and easy to remember.
- Use relevant keywords in your name or bio to improve search visibility.
- Include a call to action in your bio to encourage engagement.

2. Use a Consistent Visual Style

- Stick to a specific color palette or theme for your profile.
- Maintain consistency in post formatting and filter choices.
- Arrange Highlights into visually appealing categories.

3. Regularly Update Your Story Highlights

- Keep your most important Stories easily accessible.
- Use Highlight covers that match your brand aesthetic.

4. Engage With Followers

- Respond to comments and messages.
- Like and comment on followers' posts to build relationships.
- Use interactive stickers in Stories to encourage participation.

5. Monitor Insights for Performance Tracking

- Use Instagram Insights to analyze which posts perform best.
- Adjust your strategy based on audience engagement trends.

Conclusion

Your Instagram profile page is the foundation of your online presence. By customizing your settings, optimizing your bio and content, and maintaining a consistent aesthetic, you can enhance your Instagram experience and build a strong personal or brand identity. Whether you are a casual user or an aspiring influencer, mastering your profile settings will set you up for success.

2.3 Customizing Your Profile

2.3.1 Choosing the Right Profile Picture

Why Your Profile Picture Matters

Your Instagram profile picture is one of the most important elements of your profile. It is the first thing people notice when they visit your page, and it appears next to your username in search results, comments, and direct messages. A well-chosen profile picture helps you establish a strong first impression, conveys your brand identity, and makes your profile easily recognizable.

Whether you are using Instagram for personal, professional, or business purposes, selecting the right profile picture is crucial for increasing engagement and attracting the right audience.

Key Characteristics of an Effective Profile Picture

When choosing a profile picture, consider the following factors:

1. Clarity and High Resolution

- Use a high-quality image that is sharp and clear.
- Avoid blurry, pixelated, or heavily filtered images.
- Ensure that the image is well-lit and not too dark.

2. Recognizability

- For personal accounts, use a close-up of your face rather than a full-body shot.
- For businesses or brands, use a logo or a brand-related image.
- Keep the image simple and uncluttered so it is easily identifiable even in a small size.

3. Proper Sizing and Cropping

- Instagram profile pictures are displayed as circles, so ensure that the important parts of the image are centered.

- Use an image size of at least 320x320 pixels for optimal clarity.

- Avoid cropping out essential parts of the image, such as your face or logo.

4. Consistency with Your Brand Identity

- If you are using Instagram for business, ensure that your profile picture aligns with your brand colors and aesthetics.

- Use the same profile picture across different social media platforms to maintain consistency.

- If you are an influencer or public figure, use a professional headshot that reflects your personality.

5. Contrast and Visibility

- Choose a background that contrasts well with the subject so that it stands out.

- Avoid using overly busy backgrounds that may distract from the main focus.

- If your brand has a specific color scheme, incorporate those colors subtly.

Step-by-Step Guide to Choosing the Perfect Profile Picture

Step 1: Define Your Purpose

Before selecting a profile picture, determine what message you want to convey. Are you using Instagram for personal networking, professional branding, or business promotion? Your choice of image should align with this goal.

Step 2: Take or Select a High-Quality Image

- If using a personal photo, take a clear headshot with a clean background.

- If using a business logo, ensure it is high-resolution and properly formatted for Instagram.

- Consider hiring a professional photographer if you want a polished and professional look.

Step 3: Edit for Optimal Presentation

- Use simple editing tools to enhance brightness, contrast, and sharpness.

- Avoid excessive filters that can make the image look unnatural.

- Crop the image to ensure that the focal point is centered and clearly visible.

Step 4: Test Different Options

- Upload different profile pictures and see how they appear on your profile.

- Ask for feedback from friends, colleagues, or audience members.

- Ensure that your picture remains recognizable even in small sizes.

Common Mistakes to Avoid

- **Using a Group Photo:** This makes it difficult for people to identify you.

- **Choosing a Low-Quality Image:** A blurry or pixelated image reduces professionalism.

- **Ignoring Instagram's Circular Crop:** Parts of your image may get cut off if not properly centered.

- **Frequent Changes:** Consistency is key; changing your profile picture too often may confuse followers.

Examples of Great Profile Pictures

For **Personal Users:** A well-lit, smiling headshot with a neutral background. For **Influencers:** A stylized photo that reflects their niche and personality. For **Businesses:** A clean, high-resolution company logo that matches brand colors.

Final Thoughts

Your Instagram profile picture serves as your digital identity. It should be clear, recognizable, and aligned with your brand. By carefully selecting an image that represents you or your business effectively, you can make a strong first impression and enhance your presence on Instagram. Take the time to choose wisely and ensure your profile picture sets the right tone for your account.

2.3.2 Writing an Engaging Bio

Introduction

Your Instagram bio is one of the first things people see when they visit your profile. It serves as your digital introduction and gives visitors a quick idea of who you are and what they can expect from your account. Whether you are using Instagram for personal branding, business, or simply for fun, crafting a compelling and engaging bio is essential to make a lasting impression. This section will guide you through the key elements of a great bio and provide practical tips for optimizing yours.

Understanding the Importance of an Instagram Bio

Why Your Bio Matters

- **First Impressions Count**: Your bio is often the deciding factor in whether someone follows you or not.

- **Defines Your Brand Identity**: Whether personal or business, your bio should reflect your personality or brand.

- **Enhances Discoverability**: A well-structured bio with keywords can help people find you.

- **Encourages Engagement**: A compelling bio can motivate visitors to interact with your content or follow a call to action (CTA).

Character Limit and Constraints

Instagram bios are limited to 150 characters, so every word counts. You must be concise, engaging, and informative all at once.

Key Elements of a Great Instagram Bio

1. Your Name and Username

- **Use a recognizable name**: If you are a business, use your brand name. If personal, use your real name or a unique variation.

- **Consider including keywords**: If your username isn't clear enough, add clarifying words (e.g., "JohnDoe_Travel" instead of "JohnDoe").

2. A Clear and Concise Description

- Define who you are and what you do in one or two lines.

- Use engaging language to make it interesting.
- Examples:
  - **For Personal Brands**: "Fitness coach helping you get in shape without the gym. DM for coaching!"
  - **For Businesses**: "Handcrafted jewelry made with love. ❁ Shop our latest collection below!"

3. Emojis for Visual Appeal

- Use emojis strategically to break up text and add personality.
- Examples:
  - Travel Blogger: "✈️-□ Exploring the world, one city at a time! □"
  - Food Blogger: "🍕 | 🍣 | ☕ Food lover & recipe creator!"

4. Call to Action (CTA)

- Encourage visitors to take action, such as visiting your website, subscribing, or contacting you.
- Examples:
  - "🎥 Watch my latest vlog! Link below."
  - "✉️ DM for collaborations."

5. Link in Bio

- Use the website field for important links.
- Tools like **Linktree** or **Beacons** allow you to include multiple links in one place.

How to Craft the Perfect Bio

Step 1: Define Your Purpose

Ask yourself:

- Who is my target audience?

- What do I want people to know about me in a few seconds?

- What action do I want them to take?

Step 2: Choose the Right Tone

- Keep it casual for personal profiles.

- Maintain a professional tone for businesses.

- Be witty and creative if you want to stand out.

Step 3: Make Use of Formatting

- Use line breaks for readability (tip: draft your bio in Notes and copy-paste).

- Mix uppercase and lowercase letters for emphasis.

Example:

☐ Travel Blogger | 🔎 Currently: Bali

☐ Sharing travel tips & stunning locations

✉ DM for collabs | 🔗 New blog post below!

Examples of Instagram Bios for Different Niches

1. Personal Brand/Influencer

🚀 Growth Mindset | 📖 Lifelong Learner
Helping you achieve success in business & life
✉ DM for coaching sessions
🔗 New YouTube video out now!

2. Business (E-commerce/Store)

✨ Handcrafted candles made with love ☐
🌿 Eco-friendly & cruelty-free
🎁 Worldwide shipping | Shop now!
🔗 Order via link below

3. Content Creator

🎥 Filmmaker & Photographer
☐ Capturing life's best moments
💡 Tips & tricks for beginners
✉ DM for bookings!

4. Fitness Trainer

☐☐♂☐ Certified Personal Trainer
🔥 Helping you get stronger & healthier
💪 DM for coaching | Online programs available
🔗 Get my free meal plan!

Common Mistakes to Avoid

1. **Being Too Vague**: A bio that says "Love life! 💔" doesn't tell visitors anything useful.

2. **Using Too Many Emojis**: While emojis can be fun, overusing them makes your bio hard to read.

3. **No Call to Action**: Without a CTA, visitors might not know what to do next.

4. **Exceeding Character Limit**: Keep it concise and impactful.

5. **Using Complex Language**: Simple and direct bios are more effective.

Final Thoughts

Your Instagram bio is a powerful tool for making a great first impression and engaging your audience. By crafting a compelling bio that includes a clear description, emojis, a CTA, and a relevant link, you can make your profile more attractive and effective.

Take time to experiment and update your bio as your brand, interests, or business evolves. With the right approach, your Instagram bio can help you connect with your audience, grow your following, and achieve your goals on the platform.

Now, it's your turn! Go ahead and write your perfect Instagram bio today!

2.3.3 Adding Links and Contact Information

Why Adding Links and Contact Information Matters

Your Instagram profile is more than just a social media page; it's a gateway for people to connect with you, explore your work, or learn more about your business. Whether you're a personal user, content creator, or business owner, having well-placed links and clear contact information enhances your profile's effectiveness. It allows followers to engage with you outside Instagram, increasing brand awareness, website traffic, and customer inquiries.

Where You Can Add Links on Instagram

Instagram is known for its limited linking capabilities, but there are several places where you can effectively add links:

1. Bio Section (The Primary Link Placement)

Instagram allows users to place one clickable link in their bio. This is a crucial spot for directing traffic to your website, blog, online store, or any other external page.

How to Add a Link to Your Bio:

1. Open Instagram and go to your profile.

2. Tap "Edit Profile."

3. Locate the "Links" section and tap "Add external link."

4. Enter the URL you want to display.

5. (Optional) Edit the title of your link for better readability.

6. Tap "Done" to save changes.

Best Practices for Bio Links:

- Use a short and clean URL to make it more visually appealing.

- Regularly update the link to match your latest content or promotions.

- If you need multiple links, consider using a link aggregator tool like **Linktree, Bio.fm, or Beacons.ai** to host several links under one URL.

2. Instagram Stories (Swipe-Up & Link Stickers)

For accounts with over 10,000 followers or those using Business or Creator accounts, Instagram previously allowed the "Swipe Up" feature for links. This has now been replaced by **Link Stickers** that anyone can use, regardless of their follower count.

How to Add a Link to Your Story:

1. Open Instagram and swipe right to access the story feature.

2. Upload or take a photo/video.

3. Tap the sticker icon (square smiley face at the top).

4. Select the "Link" sticker.

5. Enter your URL and tap "Done."

6. Resize and position the sticker for better visibility.

7. Post your story.

Tips for Maximizing Link Stickers:

- Use a call-to-action (CTA) like "Tap Here" or "Learn More" to encourage clicks.

- Make the sticker noticeable by customizing its color or placement.

- Use an engaging story design to grab attention.

3. Instagram Captions (Non-Clickable but Useful)

Although Instagram doesn't allow clickable links in post captions, you can still share URLs and direct followers to your bio link.

How to Use Links in Captions Effectively:

- Shorten URLs using tools like **Bitly** to make them easier to type.

- Use CTAs such as "Visit the link in my bio" to guide followers.

- For brand campaigns, use branded hashtags alongside the link.

4. Instagram Direct Messages (DMs)

Instagram allows clickable links in Direct Messages, making it an effective way to share personalized links with interested followers.

Best Practices for Sharing Links in DMs:

- Engage with followers first before sending links to avoid being marked as spam.

- Use DMs to provide exclusive content, event registrations, or product links.

- Automate responses using Instagram Business Suite to share links efficiently.

5. Instagram Shop and Product Tags

If you have a business selling products, Instagram Shopping allows you to tag items with direct purchase links.

How to Set Up Instagram Shopping:

1. Convert to a Business or Creator account.

2. Connect your Instagram to a **Facebook Shop** or **Commerce Manager**.

3. Upload product listings and get approved for Instagram Shopping.

4. Tag products in posts, reels, and stories for direct purchases.

Adding Contact Information on Instagram

Having clear and accessible contact information is essential for businesses, influencers, and professionals looking to connect with potential clients or followers.

Where to Add Contact Information:

1. Profile Bio

- Include an email address, phone number, or alternative contact method.

- Format it neatly to maintain a professional look (e.g., ✉ info@example.com).

2. Contact Button (For Business & Creator Accounts)

Instagram provides built-in contact options for business and creator accounts. Users can reach you via **Call, Email, or Directions** directly from your profile.

How to Enable the Contact Button:

1. Go to your Instagram profile and tap "Edit Profile."

2. Scroll to "Public Business Information" (or "Profile Information" for Creator accounts).

3. Tap "Contact Options."

4. Add your **email address, phone number, or physical address.**

5. Toggle "Display contact info" on.

6. Tap "Done" to save changes.

3. Auto-Replies in DMs

If you receive frequent inquiries, setting up **Quick Replies** can save time:

How to Set Up Quick Replies:

1. Go to "Settings" > "Business" > "Saved Replies."

2. Tap the "+" button to create a new response.

3. Enter a shortcut word (e.g., "info").

4. Write the full response message.

5. Save and use by typing the shortcut in a DM.

Optimizing Links and Contact Information for Better Engagement

1. **Use Action-Oriented Language**: Instead of "Click Here," use CTAs like "Shop Now," "Discover More," or "Get Started."

2. **Track Link Performance**: Use UTM tracking codes or tools like Google Analytics to monitor clicks and engagement.

3. **Keep Contact Info Updated**: Ensure your email, phone number, and bio links are always accurate.

4. **Leverage Highlights**: Create a dedicated Highlight for important links such as product pages, FAQs, or booking forms.

Conclusion

Adding links and contact information to your Instagram profile is crucial for increasing engagement, growing your audience, and improving accessibility. Whether you're a business owner, content creator, or influencer, effectively placing and optimizing links can significantly enhance your Instagram strategy.

By following the best practices outlined in this chapter, you'll ensure that your followers have seamless access to your external content and an easy way to reach you. Now that your profile is optimized with essential links and contact details, let's move on to the next chapter and explore how to create engaging posts that capture your audience's attention!

CHAPTER II
Posting and Engaging on Instagram

3.1 Creating Your First Post

3.1.1 Selecting and Uploading Photos/Videos

Introduction

One of the most fundamental aspects of using Instagram is posting high-quality photos and videos. Whether you're sharing a personal moment, promoting a brand, or building an online presence, the quality and relevance of your media play a significant role in engagement. In this section, we will explore how to select the best photos and videos for Instagram, optimize them for maximum impact, and upload them effectively.

Choosing the Right Photos and Videos

Before uploading, it's important to carefully select photos and videos that align with your content strategy and audience expectations. Here are a few key factors to consider:

1. Image and Video Quality

- Instagram is a visually driven platform, so high-resolution images and videos are essential.

- Recommended image resolution: 1080 x 1080 pixels for square posts, 1080 x 1350 pixels for portrait mode, and 1080 x 566 pixels for landscape mode.

- Videos should be at least 720p resolution to maintain clarity.

- Avoid blurry, pixelated, or over-compressed files.

2. Composition and Aesthetics

- Follow the **rule of thirds** to create balanced and engaging compositions.

- Ensure good lighting—natural light often works best for photos.

- Use leading lines and framing to guide the viewer's eye to the main subject.

- Maintain a consistent color scheme or filter set for a cohesive Instagram feed.

3. Subject and Content Relevance

- Choose images and videos that tell a story or resonate with your audience.

- Ensure that your content aligns with your brand, niche, or personal style.

- Avoid cluttered or distracting backgrounds unless they add to the context.

- When posting promotional content, ensure branding elements are visible but not overwhelming.

Editing Photos and Videos Before Uploading

Even great shots can benefit from minor adjustments to enhance their appeal. Instagram provides built-in editing tools, but external apps can offer more professional results.

1. Basic Editing Techniques

- Adjust **brightness, contrast, and saturation** to enhance the overall image.

- Crop or straighten the image to remove unnecessary distractions.

- Sharpen the image slightly for a more polished look.

- Use **filters sparingly**—while they can enhance aesthetics, overusing them can reduce authenticity.

2. Using Third-Party Editing Apps

Some of the best apps for professional-grade editing include:

- **Adobe Lightroom** – Great for color correction and detailed adjustments.

- **VSCO** – Offers high-quality filters and manual editing tools.

- **Snapseed** – Provides precise control over image adjustments.

- **Canva** – Useful for adding text, graphics, or overlays to your images.

3. Video Editing Essentials

- Trim unnecessary footage to keep the video concise and engaging.

- Adjust the video speed for storytelling effects (slow-motion or time-lapse).

- Add captions to make your videos accessible and engaging.

- Use apps like **InShot, CapCut, or Adobe Premiere Rush** for advanced editing.

Uploading Photos and Videos to Instagram

Once you've selected and edited your content, it's time to upload it to Instagram. Follow these steps for a seamless process:

1. Open the Instagram App

- Tap the **+ (plus) icon** at the bottom of your screen.

- Select **Post** from the available options (Post, Story, Reel, or Live).

2. Selecting Your Media

- Choose the image or video from your camera roll.

- You can select multiple images/videos by tapping **Select Multiple** (carousel posts allow up to 10 media files).

- Use Instagram's built-in cropping tool to adjust the aspect ratio.

3. Applying Filters and Adjustments

- Instagram provides a variety of filters to enhance your post.

- Use the **Edit** tab for manual adjustments like brightness, contrast, and sharpness.

- Avoid excessive filtering; subtlety is often more effective.

4. Writing an Engaging Caption

- Your caption should be relevant, concise, and engaging.

- Include a **call to action** (e.g., "Tag a friend who needs to see this!").

- Use **emojis** strategically to make your caption visually appealing.

5. Adding Hashtags and Location Tags

- Use relevant hashtags to increase discoverability (e.g., #Photography, #Travel, #Foodie).

- Include a mix of popular and niche-specific hashtags.

- Tag your location if it adds context or boosts engagement.

6. Tagging People and Brands

- If your post features others, tag them using **@username** to increase engagement.

- Brands and influencers often repost user-generated content when tagged.

7. Choosing Advanced Settings

- Enable **Alt Text** for better accessibility and SEO benefits.

- Adjust comment settings if you want to limit interactions.

- Choose whether to share your post automatically to Facebook or other linked accounts.

8. Posting Your Content

- Once everything looks perfect, tap **Share** to publish your post.

- Monitor your engagement and respond to comments promptly.

Best Practices for Posting on Instagram

1. Consistency is Key

- Post regularly to keep your audience engaged.

- Use a content calendar to plan your posts in advance.

2. Experiment with Different Content Types

- Mix photos, videos, carousel posts, and reels for variety.

- Analyze performance metrics to see what works best for your audience.

3. Engage with Your Audience

- Respond to comments and DMs to build relationships.

- Encourage user-generated content by reposting tagged images.

4. Avoid Overposting or Underposting

- Posting too frequently may overwhelm your followers, while infrequent posting can reduce engagement.

- Aim for a balanced posting schedule based on audience insights.

Conclusion

Selecting and uploading the right photos and videos is essential for a successful Instagram presence. By focusing on quality, relevance, and engagement strategies, you can create visually appealing content that resonates with your audience. In the next section, we will dive into writing captions that captivate and connect with your followers.

3.1.2 Writing Captions That Engage

Instagram is a visual-first platform, but the power of a well-written caption should never be underestimated. A compelling caption can enhance your post, provide context, encourage engagement, and build a stronger connection with your audience. In this section, we will explore how to write effective Instagram captions that not only capture attention but also drive interaction.

1. Understanding the Purpose of Captions

Before diving into writing techniques, it's essential to understand why captions matter. An engaging caption can:

- **Provide context** – Explain what your post is about or add a backstory.

- **Showcase personality** – Help you develop a unique voice and tone.

- **Encourage engagement** – Prompt likes, comments, and shares through call-to-action phrases.

- **Improve discoverability** – Utilize hashtags and keywords to increase reach.

- **Drive conversions** – Persuade users to take action, such as visiting a website or purchasing a product.

2. Structuring an Effective Instagram Caption

A well-structured caption consists of the following elements:

The Hook (First Few Words Matter Most!)

Instagram truncates captions after the first few lines, requiring users to tap "See More" to read the full text. To capture attention:

- Start with a bold statement, intriguing question, or emotional hook.

- Use emojis or capital letters sparingly to highlight important points.

- Example: "STOP scrolling! 🚨 This tip will change how you edit your photos forever!"

The Body (Deliver Value and Personality)

The body of your caption should align with your brand tone. Consider these styles:

- Informative: Share insights, tutorials, or tips.

- Storytelling: Narrate personal experiences.

- Conversational: Use casual language to engage followers.

- Inspirational: Motivate your audience.

Example of a storytelling caption: *"Two years ago, I quit my 9-to-5 job to pursue my passion. I was terrified, but I believed in my vision. Today, I'm celebrating my 100,000th follower. Thank you for being part of this journey! ❤️📷'*

Call to Action (Encourage Interaction)

A strong **Call-to-Action (CTA)** increases engagement. Use:

- Question-based CTAs: "What's your favorite travel destination? Drop it in the comments! 🌍✈️🏖️"

- Instruction-based CTAs: "Double-tap if you agree! ♥☐"

- Engagement-driven CTAs: "Tag a friend who needs to hear this today!"

3. Best Practices for Writing Engaging Captions

Keep It Concise (When Necessary)

While longer captions work well for storytelling, not every post requires a lengthy message. Sometimes, **short and witty** captions perform better. Examples:

- "Monday mood: ☕ + 📖 = 💡"

- "Living my best life, one coffee at a time. ☕♥☐"

Use Emojis Strategically

Emojis can make your caption visually appealing, express emotion, and create a friendly tone. However, don't overdo it. Use them to:

- Replace words (e.g., "Let's grab some 🍕 tonight!")

- Add emotion (e.g., "Best day ever! 🎉")

- Break up long captions for readability

Leverage Hashtags Smartly

Hashtags boost discoverability, but they should be relevant to your content. Tips for using hashtags:

- Mix popular and niche hashtags (e.g., #Travel vs. #HiddenGemsAsia)

- Place them strategically (either within the caption or as a separate comment)

- Limit to 5-10 instead of maxing out at 30

Example: *"Exploring the hidden gems of Bali 🏝️✨ #TravelDiaries #BaliAdventures #HiddenParadise"*

4. Examples of High-Performing Captions

Funny Captions

- "That awkward moment when you realize your 'casual' outfit is the fanciest one in the room. ☐♂☐😂"

- "Current mood: Pretending I have my life together. ☕🌍"

Inspirational Captions

- "Dream big. Work hard. Stay focused. You're closer than you think! ✨"

- "Every day is a fresh start. Make it count! 💪"

Engagement-Based Captions

- "Which one do you prefer: beach vacation or mountain getaway? Drop your answer below! ☐☐☐☐"

- "Caption this photo! Best one gets a shoutout! 🏆"

5. Common Mistakes to Avoid

Being Too Generic

Captions like "Nice day!" or "Love this!" are boring and do not encourage engagement. Instead, add details or emotions.

Overusing Hashtags

Hashtag stuffing (#LikeForLike #FollowMe #Instagood #Fun #BestDay #PhotoOfTheDay) looks spammy. Choose relevant ones instead.

Ignoring Grammar and Spelling

While Instagram is informal, excessive typos or lack of punctuation can make captions hard to read. Proofread before posting.

6. Final Thoughts

Captions are an essential tool for engaging your Instagram audience. Whether you're crafting a short, witty remark or a long, heartfelt story, focus on authenticity, clarity, and engagement. Experiment with different styles, use CTAs effectively, and track which captions perform best for your audience. Over time, you'll develop a unique caption style that resonates and grows your Instagram presence!

3.1.3 Using Hashtags Effectively

Hashtags play a crucial role in Instagram's ecosystem. They help categorize content, improve discoverability, and increase engagement. Understanding how to use hashtags effectively can significantly enhance your reach and visibility. In this section, we will cover the fundamentals of hashtags, their benefits, strategies for using them, and common mistakes to avoid.

Understanding Hashtags on Instagram

Hashtags are words or phrases preceded by the "#" symbol. When added to a post, they create a clickable link that groups together all posts with the same hashtag. This allows users to discover content related to specific topics. Instagram supports different types of hashtags, including:

- **Branded Hashtags** – Unique to a business, campaign, or personal brand (e.g., #NikeRunning, #MyTravelJourney).

- **Industry-Specific Hashtags** – Related to a particular niche (e.g., #DigitalMarketing, #FoodPhotography).

- **Trending Hashtags** – Popular tags that are widely used at a given time (e.g., #ThrowbackThursday, #OOTD).

- **Community Hashtags** – Used to connect like-minded users (e.g., #WritersOfInstagram, #FitnessMotivation).

- **Location-Based Hashtags** – Associated with places or events (e.g., #NYCfoodie, #LondonFashionWeek).

- **Descriptive Hashtags** – Describe the content of the post (e.g., #SunsetPhotography, #VeganRecipes).

The Benefits of Using Hashtags

Hashtags are more than just a trend; they serve multiple purposes, including:

- **Increased Visibility** – Posts with relevant hashtags appear in search results and hashtag feeds, making them accessible to a broader audience.

- **Higher Engagement Rates** – Studies show that posts with at least one hashtag receive more interactions than those without.

- **Better Content Categorization** – Hashtags help organize posts, making it easier for users to find related content.

- **Brand Awareness and Recognition** – Branded hashtags encourage user-generated content and brand advocacy.

Strategies for Using Hashtags Effectively

1. Choose the Right Hashtags

Selecting the right hashtags is critical to ensuring your content reaches the right audience. Consider the following:

- **Relevance** – Use hashtags that are directly related to your content and audience.

- **Search Volume** – Find hashtags with a balance between popularity and competition. Highly popular hashtags may be oversaturated, making it difficult for your content to stand out.

- **Specificity** – Use niche hashtags that attract a targeted audience (e.g., #MinimalistPhotography instead of just #Photography).

- **Mixing Hashtag Types** – Combine broad, niche, trending, and branded hashtags for a well-rounded approach.

2. Optimize the Number of Hashtags

Instagram allows up to 30 hashtags per post, but using all of them isn't always necessary. Studies suggest that using between **5 to 15 well-chosen hashtags** often yields the best engagement.

3. Where to Place Hashtags

- **In the Caption** – Integrating hashtags naturally into your caption can enhance readability.

- **In the First Comment** – Placing hashtags in the first comment keeps the caption clean while maintaining hashtag functionality.

- **Stories and Reels** – Use hashtag stickers or add hashtags in small text to increase reach.

4. Create and Use Branded Hashtags

If you're building a personal brand or business, consider creating a unique branded hashtag. Encourage followers to use it to foster community engagement.

5. Research and Test Performance

- Use **Instagram Insights** to track which hashtags generate the most engagement.

- Experiment with different hashtag combinations to identify what works best for your audience.

- Monitor competitor hashtags to discover new opportunities.

Common Hashtag Mistakes to Avoid

1. Using Irrelevant Hashtags

Avoid using hashtags that don't align with your content, as this can reduce engagement and appear spammy.

2. Overloading Hashtags

While Instagram allows up to 30 hashtags, using too many can clutter your post and look unprofessional. Quality over quantity is key.

3. Ignoring Trending Hashtags

Not leveraging trending hashtags can mean missing out on significant exposure opportunities.

4. Using Banned or Restricted Hashtags

Instagram sometimes bans hashtags due to misuse. Check a hashtag's status before using it to avoid limiting your post's reach.

5. Being Inconsistent

Consistency in hashtag usage helps build brand recognition. Develop a hashtag strategy and stick to it.

Conclusion

Mastering the art of hashtag usage can elevate your Instagram presence, increase engagement, and expand your reach. By carefully selecting relevant hashtags, balancing their quantity, and regularly testing their effectiveness, you can maximize your Instagram growth and visibility. Implement these strategies, stay updated on trends, and refine your approach over time for optimal results.

Example 1: Using a Mix of Hashtag Types

Imagine you are a **travel blogger** posting a stunning photo of a sunset at Santorini, Greece. Instead of just using general hashtags like **#travel**, you can combine different types of hashtags for better engagement:

Post Caption:

"Golden hour in Santorini 🌅✨ Nothing beats watching the sun dip below the horizon in this magical place! Who else loves Greece? GR🖤 #SantoriniSunset #TravelMore #Wanderlust"

Hashtags Used:

- **Branded Hashtag**: #MyTravelJourney
- **Industry-Specific Hashtag**: #TravelPhotography
- **Trending Hashtag**: #GoldenHour
- **Community Hashtag**: #BackpackersLife
- **Location-Based Hashtag**: #SantoriniGreece
- **Descriptive Hashtag**: #SunsetLover

By mixing different hashtag types, your post reaches various audiences, from general travel lovers to specific Santorini tourists.

Example 2: Hashtag Placement in Caption vs. Comment

Scenario:

A **fitness influencer** posts a workout video and wants to use hashtags without making the caption look messy.

Option 1: Hashtags in Caption

"Morning workout done! 💪💦 Starting the day with energy and positivity. Who else got their workout in? #FitnessMotivation #WorkoutDone #HealthyLife"

Option 2: Hashtags in the First Comment

Caption:
"Morning workout done! 💪🔥 *Starting the day with energy and positivity. Who else got their workout in?"*

First Comment:
"#FitnessMotivation #WorkoutDone #HealthyLife #FitLife #NoExcuses #MorningRoutine"

💡 **Pro Tip**: Placing hashtags in the first comment keeps your caption clean while still making your post discoverable.

Example 3: Testing Different Hashtags

A **food blogger** posts an image of homemade vegan pancakes and tests two sets of hashtags to see which works better.

Post Caption:

"Fluffy vegan pancakes topped with fresh berries and maple syrup! Who wants a bite? 🥞🍓 *#PlantBasedEats"*

Set A (Broad Hashtags)

#Foodie #Delicious #Yummy #Breakfast #HealthyEating

Set B (Niche Hashtags)

#VeganPancakes #DairyFreeLiving #PlantBasedFoodie #HealthyBrunch #HomemadeMeals

After testing, they find that **Set B** attracts more engagement because it targets a specific audience.

Example 4: Avoiding Banned Hashtags

A **fashion influencer** posts an outfit photo and mistakenly uses **#BeautyBlogger**, which Instagram has banned due to excessive spam.

⊘ **Banned Hashtag Example:**

"Loving this summer dress! ☀☐▮ #OOTD #BeautyBlogger"

✅ **Better Alternative:**

"Loving this summer dress! ☀☐▮ #OOTD #StyleInspo #FashionGoals"

💡 **Tip**: Before using a hashtag, search for it on Instagram to ensure it's not banned or restricted.

3.1.4 Tagging People and Locations

Introduction to Tagging on Instagram

Tagging people and locations on Instagram is an essential feature that enhances engagement, increases visibility, and helps connect with others in the Instagram community. Whether you are sharing personal moments, promoting a brand, or increasing the reach of your content, tagging plays a crucial role in making your posts more discoverable. This section explores how to effectively tag people and locations in your Instagram posts, stories, and reels.

Why Tagging Matters

Tagging people and locations serves several purposes:

- **Boosts Engagement** – Posts with tagged users and locations tend to receive higher engagement as they appear in more feeds.

- **Enhances Discoverability** – Location tags help users find your posts when searching for specific places.

- **Improves Networking** – Tagging people allows for better interaction and collaboration with friends, influencers, or brands.

- **Encourages User Interaction** – When tagged, users receive notifications, increasing the chances of them engaging with your content.

Tagging People in Posts

Tagging people in an Instagram post is straightforward, and it offers numerous benefits, from giving credit to collaborators to increasing visibility. Here's how to do it:

How to Tag People in a Post

1. **Create a New Post** – Select a photo or video you want to share.

2. **Edit Your Post** – Apply filters, adjust brightness, and enhance your content as needed.

3. **Tap "Tag People"** – Before publishing your post, tap the "Tag People" option.

4. **Select a Person** – Tap on any area of the image and type the username of the person you want to tag.

5. **Confirm the Tag** – Once you find the correct user, select their profile and confirm.

6. **Publish Your Post** – Finish writing your caption, add hashtags if needed, and tap "Share."

Best Practices for Tagging People

- **Tag Relevant Users** – Only tag people who are genuinely part of the post to avoid spam-like behavior.

- **Avoid Over-Tagging** – Instagram may flag posts with excessive tags as spam.

- **Ensure Accuracy** – Always double-check usernames before tagging.

- **Ask for Permission** – If tagging a brand or influencer, it's best to ask first.

Tagging People in Stories

Instagram Stories provide an excellent way to tag users interactively. Unlike post tags, tagged users in stories can reshare the content, further increasing reach.

How to Tag Someone in a Story

1. **Open Instagram Stories** – Swipe right from your home feed or tap your profile picture.

2. **Select or Capture Content** – Choose an image or video from your gallery or take a new one.

3. **Tap the Text Tool (@Mention)** – Type "@" followed by the username of the person you want to tag.

4. **Customize the Tag** – Resize, reposition, and change the color of the tag for better visibility.

5. **Share Your Story** – Once satisfied, tap "Your Story" to post it.

Best Practices for Story Tags

- **Use Mention Stickers** – Instagram offers stylish mention stickers to make tags more appealing.

- **Tag Businesses or Influencers** – If featuring a product or collaborating, tagging increases credibility and potential resharing.

- **Ensure Visibility** – Place the tag where it's easy to read and not obstructed by other elements.

Tagging Locations in Instagram Posts

Adding a location to your post can significantly enhance its visibility and engagement. Location tags make your posts appear in location-based searches, helping users discover content related to a particular place.

How to Add a Location to a Post

1. **Create a New Post** – Select an image or video and proceed with editing.

2. **Tap "Add Location"** – Below the caption section, select the "Add Location" option.

3. **Search for a Location** – Type the name of the place you want to tag.

4. **Select the Correct Location** – Choose from Instagram's suggested places.

5. **Publish Your Post** – Finish writing your caption and tap "Share."

Best Practices for Location Tags

- **Use Specific Locations** – Instead of broad locations (e.g., "New York"), use specific places (e.g., "Central Park, NYC").

- **Tag Popular Locations** – This increases the chances of getting discovered in search results.

- **Ensure Accuracy** – Double-check the location before posting.
- **Combine with Hashtags** – Using relevant hashtags along with location tags can further improve reach.

Tagging Locations in Instagram Stories

Tagging locations in stories helps attract viewers who search for content related to a specific place.

How to Add a Location Tag in Stories

1. **Open Instagram Stories** – Swipe right from the home screen.
2. **Select or Capture Content** – Choose an image/video or take a new one.
3. **Tap the Sticker Icon** – Select the "Location" sticker from the options.
4. **Search for a Location** – Type the name of the place and select it from the list.
5. **Resize and Place the Sticker** – Adjust the sticker's position and size.
6. **Share Your Story** – Tap "Your Story" to publish it.

Best Practices for Location Tags in Stories

- **Use Trending Locations** – If a location is currently popular, tagging it can increase views.
- **Ensure Visibility** – Make sure the tag is readable and well-placed.
- **Combine with Other Features** – Adding GIFs, hashtags, or stickers can make the story more engaging.

Tagging in Instagram Reels

Instagram Reels allow users to tag people and locations just like posts and stories.

How to Tag People and Locations in Reels

1. **Create a Reel** – Record or upload video clips.
2. **Tap "Tag People"** – Before sharing, select the "Tag People" option.

3. **Tap "Add Location"** – Choose a location to increase discoverability.

4. **Finalize and Share** – Adjust captions, hashtags, and publish your reel.

Best Practices for Reels Tags

- **Tag Featured Users** – If collaborating with others, tag them to ensure proper credit.

- **Use Specific Locations** – Helps attract local audiences and engagement.

- **Encourage Sharing** – Tagged users may reshare, boosting reach.

Conclusion

Tagging people and locations on Instagram is a simple yet powerful way to expand your reach, enhance engagement, and connect with a larger audience. By effectively using tags in posts, stories, and reels, you can boost visibility, build a strong online presence, and increase interactions. Follow best practices to ensure proper tagging etiquette and maximize the benefits of this feature.

3.2 Instagram Stories: A Complete Guide

3.2.1 How to Create and Share Stories

Introduction to Instagram Stories

Instagram Stories is one of the most powerful features on the platform, allowing users to share photos and videos that disappear after 24 hours. Unlike regular posts that stay on your profile permanently (unless deleted), Stories offer a more casual, real-time way to engage with your audience. They appear in a slideshow format and can be enhanced with interactive elements such as stickers, polls, and links.

This section will guide you step-by-step on how to create and share Stories, ensuring you make the most out of this feature.

How to Create an Instagram Story

Step 1: Accessing the Stories Camera

To create an Instagram Story, follow these simple steps:

1. **Open Instagram:** Ensure you are logged into your account.

2. **Swipe right on your home screen** or tap the **'+' button** at the top left corner and select **'Story'**.

3. This will open the **Instagram Stories camera**, where you can take photos, record videos, or upload media from your gallery.

Step 2: Capturing Content

Once you have accessed the Stories camera, you can create content in several ways:

- **Tap the shutter button** to take a photo.

- **Hold the shutter button** to record a video (up to 15 seconds per segment).

- **Swipe up** to access your gallery and choose an existing photo or video.

- **Use Boomerang Mode** to create short, looping videos.

- **Select 'Hands-Free'** mode for easy recording without holding the button.

- **Use the 'Multi-Capture' feature** to take multiple photos at once.

Step 3: Adding Creative Elements

To make your Story more engaging, Instagram provides several tools:

1. Filters and Effects

- Swipe left or right to apply different filters.
- Tap on the **sparkle icon** to explore AR effects.

2. Text and Stickers

- Tap the **'Aa'** icon to add text.
- Choose from different fonts, colors, and styles.
- Use stickers (GIFs, polls, questions, and emojis) by tapping the **sticker icon**.

3. Drawing and Markup

- Tap the **pencil icon** to draw on your Story.
- Select from various brush styles and colors.

4. Adding Music

- Tap the **music sticker** to select a song.
- Choose the section of the song that fits your Story.

5. Using Links and Calls-to-Action

- If you have **10,000+ followers or a verified account**, you can add a **Swipe-Up Link**.
- For other users, use the **'Link Sticker'** to direct followers to external websites.

Sharing Your Instagram Story

Step 1: Posting Your Story

Once you're satisfied with your Story:

1. Tap the **'Your Story'** button to share it with all your followers.
2. Tap **'Close Friends'** to share it with a specific group of people.

3. Select **'Send To'** if you want to share it directly with specific users.

Step 2: Managing Story Visibility

- Go to **Settings > Privacy > Story** to customize who can see your Stories.

- You can **hide Stories from specific users** or allow **only close friends** to view them.

- Enable **Story Replies** to let followers respond via direct messages.

Step 3: Saving and Archiving Stories

- After posting, tap **'More'** (three dots) and select **'Save'** to keep a copy on your phone.

- Use **Story Highlights** to save Stories permanently on your profile.

- Access archived Stories via **Settings > Archive**.

Tips for Creating Engaging Stories

1. Keep It Authentic

- Share behind-the-scenes moments, daily updates, or personal insights.

- Avoid over-editing; raw, unfiltered content often performs better.

2. Utilize Interactive Features

- Use **polls**, **question stickers**, and **quizzes** to engage with your audience.

- Add **countdown timers** for product launches or special events.

3. Post Consistently

- Aim to post Stories daily to stay visible in followers' feeds.

- Plan content in advance using Instagram's **Content Calendar**.

4. Use Analytics to Improve

- Check **Instagram Insights** to see how your Stories are performing.

- Adjust content based on **completion rate**, **views**, and **engagement levels**.

Conclusion

Instagram Stories is a versatile tool for both casual users and businesses. By mastering the creation and sharing process, you can enhance engagement, grow your audience, and improve your online presence. Whether you're using Stories to share personal updates or promote your brand, implementing these best practices will ensure your content stands out.

Now that you know how to create and share Stories, the next section will cover **Instagram Reels**, another powerful way to connect with your audience!

3.2.2 Adding Stickers, Polls, and Interactive Elements

Instagram Stories offer a dynamic way to engage with your audience, and one of the most effective methods is through interactive elements such as stickers, polls, questions, countdowns, and quizzes. These features enhance user engagement, increase visibility, and foster community interactions. This section will cover how to add and effectively use these elements in your Instagram Stories.

Understanding Instagram Stickers

Stickers are a versatile tool in Instagram Stories, offering both decorative and functional benefits. They help convey messages, encourage engagement, and personalize content.

How to Add Stickers to Your Story

1. **Create a Story**: Open Instagram, tap the **"Your Story"** icon, and either take a photo, record a video, or upload one from your gallery.

2. **Access the Sticker Tray**: Tap the **smiley face sticker icon** at the top of the screen.

3. **Choose a Sticker**: Browse through the available stickers and select one that fits your content.

4. **Customize and Place the Sticker**: Resize, rotate, or move the sticker to your preferred position on the Story.

5. **Share Your Story**: Tap **"Your Story"** to publish it.

Popular Types of Stickers

- **Location Sticker**: Tags your current location, increasing discoverability.

- **Hashtag Sticker**: Allows users to explore related content under the tagged hashtag.

- **Mention Sticker**: Tags another Instagram user, notifying them and increasing engagement.

- **Time and Date Stickers**: Automatically display the current time or date.

- **GIF Stickers**: Add animated elements to make your Stories more visually appealing.

- **Music Sticker**: Enables you to add a song to your Story for a more immersive experience.

Using Polls to Engage Your Audience

Poll stickers allow you to ask questions with two response options. This is a great way to gauge opinions, spark discussions, or simply entertain your followers.

How to Add a Poll

1. **Open the Sticker Tray** and select the **Poll** sticker.

2. **Type Your Question**: Keep it concise and engaging.

3. **Set Answer Choices**: The default is "Yes" and "No," but you can customize them.

4. **Position the Poll**: Drag and resize it for better visibility.

5. **Share and Track Results**: Once your Story is live, track votes in the Story insights.

Best Practices for Polls

- Use **simple and clear questions** to encourage participation.

- Make polls **fun and engaging**, such as "Which outfit should I wear today?"

- Utilize polls for **market research**, asking for feedback on products or ideas.

- Increase **interactivity** by using polls before revealing a surprise or answer.

Adding Questions for Deeper Interaction

Question stickers allow followers to submit responses, making your Stories more interactive.

How to Use the Question Sticker

1. **Select the Question Sticker** from the sticker tray.

2. **Customize the Prompt**: The default text is "Ask me a question," but you can edit it.

3. **Encourage Responses**: Use clear and inviting wording.

4. **Share Responses**: You can publicly reply to responses without revealing usernames.

Best Practices for Questions

- Use **open-ended questions** to spark discussions.

- Ask for **opinions, experiences, or recommendations**.

- Engage followers by allowing them to **ask you anything**.

Leveraging the Countdown Sticker

The Countdown Sticker is perfect for creating excitement about an upcoming event, sale, or announcement.

How to Use the Countdown Sticker

1. **Select the Countdown Sticker** from the sticker tray.

2. **Set a Name and Date/Time** for your countdown.

3. **Customize the Look** by changing colors and fonts.

4. **Encourage Followers to Subscribe** to get a notification when the countdown ends.

Best Practices for Countdowns

- **Build anticipation** for new product launches or events.
- **Use reminders** to keep followers engaged.
- **Promote urgency** for limited-time offers.

Using Emoji Sliders for Fun Engagement

The emoji slider allows users to express their reactions on a scale.

How to Add an Emoji Slider

1. **Choose the Emoji Slider** from the sticker menu.
2. **Type Your Question or Prompt**.
3. **Select an Emoji** that matches the sentiment.
4. **Post and Monitor Responses**.

Best Uses for Emoji Sliders

- Gauge excitement levels (e.g., "How excited are you for this event?").
- Gather feedback on content or ideas.
- Add a playful touch to your Stories.

Interactive Quizzes for Engagement

Quiz stickers let you create multiple-choice questions where followers can select the correct answer.

How to Use the Quiz Sticker

1. **Select the Quiz Sticker**.
2. **Write Your Question** and add multiple-choice answers.

3. **Choose the Correct Answer**.

4. **Customize the Look**.

5. **Post and Track Responses**.

Best Uses for Quiz Stickers

- Educational content (e.g., "Do you know this fun fact?").

- Brand storytelling (e.g., "Which year was our company founded?").

- Product-related quizzes (e.g., "Which product feature do you like most?").

Conclusion

Adding interactive elements like stickers, polls, and questions to Instagram Stories transforms passive viewers into engaged participants. These tools not only enhance the visual appeal of your content but also help build a more connected and loyal audience. Experiment with different features to find what resonates best with your followers and maximize engagement on your Stories.

3.2.3 Highlights: Saving Your Best Stories

Introduction to Instagram Highlights

Instagram Stories disappear after 24 hours, but what if you want to keep your best moments visible for longer? That's where **Instagram Highlights** come in. Highlights allow you to save and categorize your favorite Stories on your profile, making them permanently accessible to your audience. They act as curated collections that help visitors quickly understand who you are, what you offer, and why they should follow you.

This section will guide you through everything you need to know about Instagram Highlights, from creating and organizing them to optimizing them for engagement and branding.

Why Use Instagram Highlights?

Instagram Highlights are more than just saved Stories; they are an essential tool for branding, storytelling, and engagement. Here's why you should use them:

- **Extend the Life of Your Stories** – Normally, Stories disappear after 24 hours. Highlights keep them permanently visible.

- **Showcase Your Best Content** – Use Highlights to feature your best work, whether it's product demos, testimonials, FAQs, or important updates.

- **Improve Profile Aesthetics** – Custom Highlight covers make your profile look more professional and cohesive.

- **Organize Information Efficiently** – Categorize content into different Highlights to make it easier for visitors to find what they need.

- **Increase Engagement** – When users find value in your Highlights, they are more likely to engage with your content and follow you.

How to Create Instagram Highlights

Step 1: Access Your Archived Stories

By default, Instagram automatically saves your Stories in the **Archive** section. To access them:

1. Open Instagram and go to your profile.

2. Tap the **three-line menu** (top right corner) and select **Archive**.

3. You will see all your past Stories arranged by date.

Step 2: Create a New Highlight

1. On your profile, tap the **"+ New"** button under the bio section.

2. Select the Stories you want to add to this Highlight.

3. Tap **Next** and enter a name for your Highlight.

4. Choose a cover image (either from the selected Stories or upload a custom design).

5. Tap **Add**, and your Highlight will appear on your profile.

Step 3: Edit and Update Highlights

To edit an existing Highlight:

1. Go to your profile and tap on the Highlight you want to edit.

2.   Tap the **More (three dots)** button in the bottom right corner.

3.   Select **Edit Highlight**.

4.   Add or remove Stories, change the title, or update the cover image.

5.   Tap **Done** to save changes.

Best Practices for Instagram Highlights

1. Organize Highlights by Category

Keep your Highlights structured and easy to navigate. Here are some category ideas:

- **About Me** – Introduce yourself or your brand.

- **Products/Services** – Showcase your offerings.

- **Testimonials** – Feature customer reviews and feedback.

- **Tutorials** – Share how-to guides and demos.

- **Events** – Save highlights from special occasions.

- **Behind-the-Scenes** – Give followers an exclusive look at your process.

2. Use Custom Highlight Covers

Custom Highlight covers help create a polished and professional look. Tips for designing covers:

- Use consistent colors and fonts that match your branding.

- Keep icons simple and clear.

- Use Canva or Adobe Spark to create aesthetic covers.

- Ensure readability, even at small sizes.

3. Update Highlights Regularly

Don't let your Highlights become outdated. Regularly refresh them by:

- Removing irrelevant or old content.

- Adding new Stories that align with your current strategy.

- Reordering Highlights based on importance.

4. Keep Titles Short and Clear

Highlight titles should be concise yet informative. Examples:

- "Shop Now"
- "Tips & Tricks"
- "Q&A"
- "Reviews"
- "BTS" (Behind the Scenes)

5. Encourage Viewers to Check Highlights

Actively direct followers to your Highlights by:

- Mentioning them in your Stories (e.g., "Check out my Highlights for more details!")
- Including a CTA in captions (e.g., "Tap my Highlights for exclusive content!")
- Using Stories to promote a new Highlight update.

Advanced Strategies for Instagram Highlights

1. Highlight Sequences for Storytelling

Instead of random Stories, create Highlights that tell a story in a sequence. For example:

- **Launch Story:** Introduce a new product.
- **Demo Story:** Show how it works.
- **Customer Review Story:** Feature user feedback.
- **Call-to-Action Story:** Direct followers to purchase.

2. Use Highlights for Sales and Promotions

If you run a business, Highlights can act as a **mini storefront**:

- Feature current promotions.

- Provide a catalog of products with links to shop.

- Share discount codes.

3. Optimize Highlights for SEO

Instagram allows searches within Highlights. Use relevant **keywords** in Highlight titles and descriptions to boost discoverability.

4. Leverage Highlights for Influencer Collaborations

If you work with influencers, save collaborations in a dedicated Highlight:

- Showcase their testimonials.

- Feature them using your product.

- Share joint campaigns.

5. Use Polls and Q&A Stories in Highlights

Keep interactive elements like polls, quizzes, and Q&A sessions in Highlights to boost engagement.

Common Mistakes to Avoid

1. **Cluttering Highlights with Too Many Stories** – Keep them concise and relevant.

2. **Inconsistent Cover Design** – Use a uniform theme to maintain a professional look.

3. **Forgetting to Update Highlights** – Regularly refresh content to keep it relevant.

4. **Not Using CTAs** – Encourage viewers to take action (e.g., visit website, shop, follow).

Conclusion

Instagram Highlights are a powerful tool to enhance your profile, engage followers, and showcase important content. By strategically organizing, designing, and updating your Highlights, you can make a lasting impression on visitors and drive more engagement on your account.

Start curating your Instagram Highlights today and turn your profile into a well-structured, engaging space for your audience!

Example 1: Small Business Using Highlights for Marketing

Scenario:
Emma owns a small handmade jewelry business. She wants to use Instagram Highlights to help potential customers quickly browse her products and learn about her brand.

How She Uses Highlights:

- **"New Arrivals"** – Features the latest jewelry pieces with pricing and descriptions.
- **"Customer Reviews"** – Showcases testimonials from happy customers wearing her jewelry.
- **"How It's Made"** – Behind-the-scenes videos of her making jewelry by hand.
- **"Special Offers"** – Displays ongoing discounts or promotions with links to shop.

Result:
Her Highlights make it easy for new visitors to explore her brand, increasing engagement and driving more sales.

Example 2: Fitness Coach Engaging Clients with Highlights

Scenario:
Jake is a fitness coach who wants to provide useful content to his followers while also promoting his training services.

How He Uses Highlights:

- **"Workout Tips"** – Short videos of him demonstrating exercises with tips on proper form.
- **"Client Transformations"** – Before-and-after photos of clients who followed his workout plans.
- **"Meal Plans"** – Healthy meal ideas with calorie breakdowns.
- **"Q&A"** – Answers to commonly asked fitness questions.

Result:

His followers get quick access to valuable fitness content, building trust and encouraging them to sign up for his coaching programs.

Example 3: Influencer Showcasing Collaborations

Scenario:

Sophie is a beauty influencer who collaborates with various skincare brands. She wants to use Instagram Highlights to showcase her partnerships and recommendations.

How She Uses Highlights:

- **"Skincare Routines"** – Step-by-step videos of her morning and evening skincare routine using different products.

- **"Brand Collabs"** – Reviews and discount codes for brands she partners with.

- **"Makeup Tutorials"** – Short clips of her creating different makeup looks.

- **"Behind the Scenes"** – BTS footage of her photoshoots and influencer events.

Result:

Her Highlights keep her profile organized while providing value to her audience, making her a more attractive partner for brands.

Example 4: Restaurant Showcasing Menu & Customer Feedback

Scenario:

A local café wants to make it easier for Instagram visitors to see their menu, promotions, and customer experiences.

How They Use Highlights:

- **"Menu"** – Photos of their dishes with prices.

- **"Happy Customers"** – Reposted Instagram Stories from customers who tag the café.

- **"Events & Specials"** – Upcoming live music nights, holiday promotions, and seasonal dishes.

- **"Behind-the-Scenes"** – Clips of the chefs preparing meals.

Result:
New customers can quickly see what the café offers and feel encouraged to visit.

Example 5: Travel Blogger Organizing Destination Highlights

Scenario:
Lucas is a travel blogger who wants to organize his trips so followers can easily find travel recommendations.

How He Uses Highlights:

- **"Bali"** – Best places to visit, eat, and stay in Bali.

- **"Paris"** – Instagrammable spots and hidden gems in Paris.

- **"Budget Travel Tips"** – Advice on how to travel affordably.

- **"Travel Gear"** – His recommended travel essentials and gadgets.

Result:
His Highlights serve as a quick travel guide for followers who are planning trips.

3.3 Understanding Instagram Reels

3.3.1 Creating Short-Form Video Content

Introduction to Short-Form Video Content

Short-form video content has taken the digital world by storm, and Instagram Reels is at the forefront of this trend. With Reels, users can create and share engaging videos of up to 90 seconds, making it an essential tool for influencers, brands, and casual users alike. Whether you want to entertain, educate, or promote, mastering Reels can significantly enhance your Instagram presence.

This section will guide you through the process of creating high-quality Reels, from conceptualizing ideas to filming, editing, and optimizing for maximum engagement.

Why Short-Form Video Matters

- **Increased Engagement:** Reels are prioritized by Instagram's algorithm, giving them a higher chance of reaching new audiences.

- **Viral Potential:** With the right strategy, Reels can gain massive visibility beyond your followers.

- **Bite-Sized Storytelling:** Short-form videos are digestible and effective for delivering messages quickly.

- **Versatility:** Perfect for tutorials, behind-the-scenes content, challenges, promotions, and more.

Step-by-Step Guide to Creating an Instagram Reel

1. Planning Your Reel

Before you start recording, take time to plan your content. Ask yourself:

- **What is the purpose of this Reel?** (Entertainment, education, promotion, etc.)

- **Who is the target audience?**

- **What message do you want to convey?**

- **What visuals and audio will best support your message?**

Consider researching trending Reels and sounds for inspiration. Look at the "Explore" and "Reels" tabs to identify popular formats and themes.

2. Recording Your Reel

To start creating a Reel, follow these steps:

1. **Open the Instagram app** and tap the "+" button, then select "Reel."

2. **Choose a recording option:**
   o Record in real-time by holding the capture button.
   o Upload pre-recorded clips from your gallery.
   o Use the "Align" tool to create seamless transitions between clips.

3. **Adjust video speed:** Instagram allows you to speed up or slow down your clips for creative effects.

4. **Set a timer and countdown:** Useful for hands-free recording and maintaining smooth transitions.

5. **Use filters and effects:** Instagram offers a variety of AR effects to enhance your video.

6. **Frame your shots properly:** Ensure good lighting and a clear focus on your subject.

7. **Use multiple angles:** Variety in perspectives makes your Reel more engaging.

3. Editing Your Reel

Once you have recorded your clips, it's time to edit. Instagram provides built-in tools for trimming, adjusting, and enhancing your video:

- **Trimming Clips:** Remove unnecessary sections to keep your video concise.

- **Reordering Clips:** Arrange them in the best sequence for storytelling.

- **Adding Text and Stickers:** Highlight important points or add humor.

- **Using Filters:** Adjust colors and mood to make your Reel visually appealing.

- **Applying Effects:** Slow motion, transitions, and other effects enhance the experience.

4. Choosing the Right Music and Sounds

Audio plays a significant role in making Reels engaging. You can:

- Select trending sounds from Instagram's library.
- Use original audio by recording your voice.
- Add voiceovers for narration.
- Sync video cuts to beats for dynamic content.

5. Writing an Engaging Caption and Hashtags

- **Keep it short and catchy.**
- **Use a call-to-action (CTA).** Example: "Tag a friend who needs to see this!"
- **Include relevant hashtags.** Helps in reaching a broader audience (e.g., #Reels, #Trending, #InstagramTips).

6. Posting and Optimizing Your Reel

Before hitting "Share," ensure you:

- Select an **eye-catching thumbnail** (choose a frame or upload a custom cover).
- Tag relevant users or brands.
- Add a location (if relevant for local engagement).
- Enable sharing to **Feed and Explore** for maximum reach.
- Engage with early commenters to boost visibility.

7. Analyzing Performance and Improving

Instagram Insights provides valuable data to refine your Reels strategy:

- **Views:** How many people watched your Reel.
- **Likes and Comments:** Engagement levels.
- **Shares and Saves:** Indicators of valuable content.
- **Watch Time:** Shows how long people stayed on your video.

Use these metrics to identify what works best and adjust your future Reels accordingly.

Pro Tips for Creating Viral Reels

- Follow trends but add originality.

- Keep it short and engaging (ideally 15-30 seconds).

- Hook viewers in the first 3 seconds.

- Use text overlays to enhance comprehension.

- Maintain a consistent posting schedule.

- Engage with viewers through comments and responses.

- Repurpose successful content from other platforms (e.g., TikTok, YouTube Shorts).

Conclusion

Mastering short-form video content on Instagram Reels can significantly enhance your social media presence. By planning, recording, editing, and optimizing your videos effectively, you can create engaging content that resonates with your audience and increases your reach.

In the next section, we will dive deeper into **Using Music, Effects, and Transitions** to make your Reels even more dynamic and engaging.

3.3.2 Using Music, Effects, and Transitions

Introduction

Instagram Reels has become one of the most powerful tools for content creators, businesses, and everyday users to engage with their audience. One of the key features that make Reels stand out is the ability to add music, effects, and transitions. These elements help enhance the storytelling aspect of your videos, making them more engaging and professional-looking. This section will guide you through everything you need to know about incorporating music, effects, and transitions into your Reels.

Adding Music to Your Instagram Reels

1. Why Music Matters

Music plays a crucial role in setting the tone and mood of your Reels. It helps grab attention, evoke emotions, and increase engagement. Whether you're creating a fun dance video, an informative tutorial, or a promotional clip, the right background music can make a significant impact.

2. How to Add Music to Your Reels

Instagram provides a built-in music library where you can browse and select tracks for your Reels. Follow these steps to add music:

1. Open Instagram and tap the **"+"** button to create a new Reel.

2. Tap **"Audio"** on the left-hand side of the screen.

3. Use the search bar to find a song or browse trending audio.

4. Tap on a track to preview it and select the part you want to use.

5. Adjust the music's volume by tapping the **audio mix** option if you also have voiceovers or original sounds.

6. Tap **Done** and proceed with recording or editing your video.

3. Using Original Audio

If you prefer to use your own sound, Instagram allows you to add original audio. Here's how:

- Record your Reel with your voice or background noise.

- Once posted, your audio will be labeled as **"Original Audio"**, allowing other users to use it in their own Reels.

- To add your voiceover, tap **"Microphone"** while editing and record your narration.

4. Copyright Considerations

Instagram has licensing agreements with music labels, but not all songs are available for business accounts. If you run a business account and can't access certain tracks, consider:

- Using royalty-free music from platforms like Epidemic Sound, Artlist, or SoundStripe.

- Uploading original music or instrumental tracks.

- Partnering with independent musicians for custom tracks.

Enhancing Your Reels with Effects

1. What Are Effects?

Effects on Instagram Reels are visual filters and augmented reality (AR) elements that can enhance your video. They range from simple color adjustments to interactive and animated overlays.

2. How to Add Effects to Your Reels

Instagram offers a variety of built-in effects. Here's how you can apply them:

1. Open Instagram and start creating a Reel.

2. Tap **"Effects"** on the left-hand side before recording.

3. Browse through the available effects or search for specific ones.

4. Tap on an effect to preview it before recording.

5. Once you've found the perfect effect, start recording your Reel.

3. Popular Effects to Try

- **Green Screen**: Allows you to replace the background with an image or video.

- **Slow Motion**: Adds a dramatic effect to movements and highlights details.

- **Beauty Filters**: Enhances facial features and smoothens skin.

- **Color Grading**: Adjusts the color tones for a cinematic look.

- **Glitch and Retro Effects**: Creates a vintage or futuristic vibe.

4. Customizing Effects

You can also create and save your own AR effects using **Spark AR Studio**, Facebook's AR creation tool. This is particularly useful for businesses or creators looking to build a unique brand identity.

Mastering Transitions for Seamless Reels

1. What Are Transitions?

Transitions are editing techniques that allow you to smoothly switch from one scene to another, making your Reel more dynamic and engaging. Well-executed transitions can make your video look professionally edited, even if it's filmed on a smartphone.

2. How to Use Transitions Effectively

There are two main ways to add transitions to your Instagram Reels:

A. In-Camera Transitions (Filming Techniques)

These transitions rely on creative filming rather than editing tools. Some popular methods include:

- **Jump Cut**: Quickly changing from one scene to another by stopping and restarting recording in a new position.

- **Hand Cover Transition**: Covering the lens with your hand and removing it in the next scene.

- **Outfit Change**: Pausing the recording, changing your outfit, and resuming from the same position.

- **Spin Transition**: Spinning your phone at the end of a scene and matching the movement in the next clip.

B. Editing Transitions (Post-Production)

You can also use Instagram's built-in editing tools or third-party apps to add transitions:

1. **Using Instagram's Built-in Features**
   - After recording, tap on **"Edit Clips"**.
   - Drag and trim clips to create a smooth flow.
   - Use the **"Align"** feature to position yourself correctly before the next clip.

2. **Using Third-Party Apps**
   - **InShot**: Provides advanced transition effects like fade, zoom, and slide.
   - **CapCut**: Offers seamless automatic transitions for professional-looking edits.
   - **VN Video Editor**: Allows for keyframe animations and custom motion effects.

3. Tips for Smooth Transitions

- Plan your transitions in advance to ensure seamless execution.

- Use a tripod or stabilize your phone to maintain consistency.

- Match movement direction between clips (e.g., if your first clip moves to the right, continue in that direction in the next clip).

- Use beats in the music as cues for transitions.

Conclusion

Using music, effects, and transitions in your Instagram Reels can significantly enhance the quality of your content and increase engagement. Whether you're using built-in features or third-party tools, understanding how to integrate these elements effectively will help you create visually compelling and professional Reels. Keep experimenting with different styles, stay updated with new Instagram features, and most importantly—have fun with your creative process!

3.3.3 Best Practices for Viral Reels

Instagram Reels is one of the most powerful tools for expanding your reach on Instagram. With its short-form, engaging video format, Reels has the potential to make your content go viral and attract thousands—or even millions—of views. But creating viral Reels requires more than just posting a video; it involves strategy, creativity, and consistency. In this section, we'll cover the best practices to help your Reels gain traction and maximize engagement.

1. Understand What Makes a Reel Go Viral

A viral Reel typically has a combination of the following elements:

- **Strong Hook**: The first 2-3 seconds should grab attention immediately.

- **High-Quality Visuals**: Clear, bright, and well-edited videos perform better.

- **Trending Sounds & Music**: Using trending audio can boost visibility.

- **Engaging Content**: The video should be entertaining, educational, or relatable.

- **Fast-Paced Editing**: Quick cuts and transitions keep viewers engaged.

- **Call-to-Action (CTA)**: Encouraging likes, comments, shares, or saves increases interaction.

2. Optimize Your Video for Maximum Engagement

Start with a Hook

The first few seconds are critical. If your video doesn't grab attention immediately, users will scroll past it. Consider starting with:

- A bold statement or question.

- A visually striking scene.

- A problem-solution format (e.g., "Struggling with productivity? Try this!").

Use High-Quality Visuals

Instagram prioritizes high-resolution, visually appealing content. Tips to improve quality:

- Film in **1080p or 4K resolution**.

- Use **good lighting** (natural light or ring lights work well).

- Avoid shaky footage (use a tripod or stabilizer if necessary).

- Edit for clarity and appeal using apps like CapCut, InShot, or Adobe Premiere Rush.

Keep It Short and Fast-Paced

Short, snappy videos tend to perform better than longer, slow-paced ones.

- Aim for **7-15 seconds** for maximum impact.

- Cut unnecessary pauses and maintain energy throughout.

- Use quick transitions to maintain viewer interest.

3. Leverage Instagram's Algorithm to Your Advantage

Instagram's algorithm favors Reels that:

- Have high watch time (people watch till the end).

- Receive high engagement (likes, shares, saves, and comments).

- Use trending audio and effects.
- Are shared multiple times (send to friends, repost in Stories, etc.).

Use Trending Audio & Music

Instagram often boosts Reels that use trending sounds. To find trending audio:

- Check the Reels Explore page.
- Look for the "Trending" arrow next to a sound.
- Save trending sounds to use later.
- Create original sounds that others can use.

Encourage Engagement

Engagement signals to Instagram that your content is valuable. Boost engagement by:

- Asking a question in your caption or video.
- Adding a call-to-action ("Double-tap if you agree!", "Tag a friend who needs this!").
- Encouraging people to remix or duet your Reel.
- Using text overlays to emphasize key points.

4. Master Hashtags and Captions for Discoverability

Choose the Right Hashtags

Using the right hashtags helps Instagram categorize your Reel and show it to the right audience.

- Mix **broad** and **niche-specific** hashtags (e.g., #ViralReels + #DigitalMarketingTips).
- Use **5-10 highly relevant hashtags**.
- Test different hashtag sets to see what works best.

Write Compelling Captions

While Reels are video-based, captions still play a role in engagement.

- Keep captions short and engaging.

- Use humor, emojis, and storytelling.

- End with a **strong CTA** (e.g., "Save this for later!").

5. Experiment, Analyze, and Improve

Post Consistently

The more Reels you post, the better Instagram understands your content. Try to:

- Post at least 3-5 Reels per week.

- Test different formats, styles, and topics.

- Analyze which Reels perform best.

Use Instagram Insights to Track Performance

Instagram provides analytics to help you understand what works.

- Check watch time and completion rate.

- Look at engagement metrics (likes, comments, shares, saves).

- Adjust your strategy based on performance data.

Conclusion

Creating viral Reels requires a mix of creativity, strategy, and consistency. By focusing on high-quality content, engaging storytelling, trending audio, and audience interaction, you can significantly increase your chances of making Reels that go viral. Keep experimenting, analyzing your performance, and refining your approach to maximize your success on Instagram.

3.4 Engaging with Others

3.4.1 Liking, Commenting, and Sharing Posts

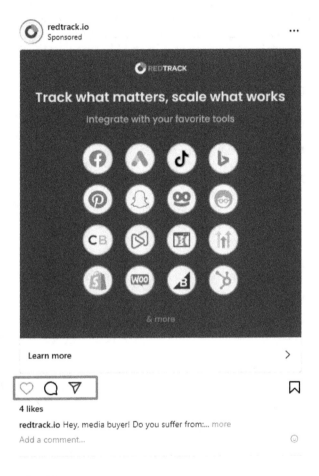

Introduction

Engagement is the key to success on Instagram. The more you interact with others, the more visible and connected your profile becomes. Instagram's engagement features—liking, commenting, and sharing—help foster connections, build relationships, and grow your presence on the platform. This section will provide a comprehensive guide to utilizing these features effectively.

Liking Posts

Understanding the Power of Likes

Liking posts is the simplest form of engagement on Instagram. When you double-tap a post or tap the heart icon, you express appreciation for the content. Though likes are no longer the primary metric for success, they still play a significant role in Instagram's algorithm.

How to Like a Post

1. Scroll through your feed and find a post you appreciate.

2. Double-tap anywhere on the image or video, or tap the heart icon below it.

3. The heart will turn red, indicating that you have liked the post.

Strategic Liking for Growth

- **Like posts from your niche**: Engaging with content in your industry helps Instagram understand your interests, increasing the chances of your content appearing in similar feeds.

- **Like posts from potential followers**: Interacting with users who share similar interests can attract them to check out your profile.

- **Be active in liking posts**: Regularly engaging with content ensures you remain visible within your network.

Avoiding Overuse of Likes

While liking is a great engagement tool, excessive liking, especially in a short period, can trigger Instagram's spam detection and result in temporary action blocks. Instead of randomly liking hundreds of posts, engage meaningfully.

Commenting on Posts

Why Comments Matter

Comments are a stronger engagement signal than likes. A well-thought-out comment can spark a conversation, build relationships, and boost visibility in Instagram's algorithm. Posts with more comments tend to be shown to a larger audience.

How to Leave a Comment

1. Open a post and tap the speech bubble icon below the image or video.

2. Type your comment in the text box.

3. Tap "Post" to share your comment.

Best Practices for Commenting

- **Be authentic**: Avoid generic comments like "Nice!" or "Great post!" Instead, personalize your comments.

- **Ask questions**: Engage the content creator by asking about their post, experience, or opinions.

- **Use emojis wisely**: Emojis add personality but should be used in moderation.

- **Tag relevant users**: If a post reminds you of someone, tag them to encourage interaction.

Commenting Strategies for Growth

- **Engage with influencers**: Commenting on posts from popular accounts in your niche increases your visibility.

- **Reply to comments on your posts**: This encourages conversations and keeps engagement levels high.

- **Join trending discussions**: Engage with popular topics and hashtags to get noticed by a broader audience.

Avoiding Spam-like Comments

Commenting "Follow for follow" or copying and pasting generic responses can make your profile appear spammy. Always add value when commenting.

Sharing Posts

Why Sharing Matters

Sharing posts helps spread valuable content while also boosting engagement. When you share another user's post, you introduce it to your followers, increasing its reach.

How to Share a Post to Your Story

1. Find a post you want to share.

2. Tap the paper airplane icon below the post.

3. Select "Add post to your story."

4. Customize the story with stickers, text, or GIFs.

5. Tap "Your Story" to share.

How to Share a Post via Direct Message (DM)

1. Tap the paper airplane icon.

2. Select the recipient(s) from your list or search for a user.

3. Add an optional message.

4. Tap "Send."

Encouraging Others to Share Your Posts

- **Create shareable content**: Infographics, quotes, and helpful tips tend to get shared more frequently.

- **Ask for shares in captions**: Politely encouraging followers to share your content increases your reach.

- **Tag people in relevant content**: If your post is relevant to specific users, tagging them can encourage them to share it.

Monitoring Shared Posts

Instagram does not provide direct notifications when someone shares your post to their story unless they tag you. However, using Instagram Insights (for business and creator accounts) allows you to track shares.

Conclusion

Liking, commenting, and sharing are essential engagement tools that contribute to building a strong Instagram presence. Using these tools strategically enhances visibility, fosters connections, and increases the chances of growth on the platform. The key is to be authentic, engaging, and consistent in your interactions. In the next section, we will explore deeper engagement methods such as direct messaging and collaborations.

3.4.2 Direct Messaging (DMs) and Chat Features

Introduction to Instagram Direct Messaging

Instagram Direct Messaging (DM) is a powerful communication tool that allows users to send private messages to individuals or groups. Unlike public posts and comments, DMs provide a private space for conversations, making them an essential feature for personal connections, networking, and customer engagement.

Whether you want to chat with friends, collaborate with influencers, or provide customer support for your business, understanding how to effectively use Instagram's DM features can enhance your overall experience on the platform.

How to Access Direct Messages

To access Instagram Direct:

1. Open the Instagram app.

2. Tap the **paper airplane icon** (or messenger icon) in the top right corner of the home screen.

3. You will see a list of conversations, including individual and group chats.

If you have connected your Instagram account with Facebook Messenger, your inbox may display an integrated messaging experience, allowing you to chat with Facebook users as well.

Sending a Direct Message

Sending a message on Instagram is straightforward:

1. Tap the **paper airplane icon** in the top right.

2. Tap the **pencil and paper icon** in the top right to start a new message.

3. Search for the username of the person you want to message.

4. Type your message and hit **Send**.

You can send various types of content via DM, including:

- Text messages

- Photos and videos

- Voice messages

- Stickers and GIFs

- Reactions to messages

- Links

- Disappearing messages (Vanishing mode)

Using Group Chats

Instagram allows you to create group chats with multiple users:

1. Open the **Direct Messages** section.

2. Tap the **pencil and paper icon** to start a new chat.

3. Select multiple users to add to the conversation.

4. Name the group and start chatting.

Group chats are great for discussions, collaborations, and community engagement. Users can react to messages, send polls, and even schedule events.

Vanishing Mode and Disappearing Messages

Instagram's Vanishing Mode allows you to send messages that disappear once they have been seen and the chat is closed. To activate Vanishing Mode:

1. Open a chat.

2. Swipe up on the conversation screen.

3. The background will turn dark, indicating that Vanishing Mode is on.

4. Any messages sent in this mode will disappear after being viewed.

This feature is useful for temporary and private conversations, but it should be used cautiously, as recipients can still take screenshots.

Sending Voice Messages

Voice messaging is a convenient way to communicate without typing. To send a voice message:

1. Open a chat.

2. Tap and hold the **microphone icon**.

3. Record your message and release the button to send.

Voice messages are commonly used for quick conversations, customer inquiries, and casual chats.

Video Calls and Audio Calls

Instagram allows users to make video and audio calls directly from the DM section:

1. Open a chat.

2. Tap the **video camera icon** or **phone icon**.

3. Wait for the recipient to answer.

Video calls can be one-on-one or group calls. They are useful for business meetings, virtual hangouts, and customer support.

Message Requests and Privacy Settings

If someone you don't follow sends you a message, it will appear in your **Message Requests** section. You can choose to:

- Accept the message and move it to your main inbox.

- Decline or block the sender.

- Report the message if it contains inappropriate content.

To manage your DM privacy settings:

1. Go to **Settings** > **Privacy** > **Messages**.

2. Choose who can send you DMs (Everyone, People You Follow, No One).

3. Customize group message settings and filtered requests.

Using Quick Replies (For Business Accounts)

Business and creator accounts can use **Quick Replies** to respond to frequently asked questions. To set up Quick Replies:

1. Go to **Settings** > **Business** > **Saved Replies**.

2. Tap **New Saved Reply**.

3. Type your frequently used response and assign a shortcut.

This feature saves time for businesses handling customer inquiries.

Reacting and Replying to Messages

Users can react to messages with emojis to express emotions quickly:

1. Long-press a message.

2. Select an emoji reaction (❤️☐😂🔥💧, etc.).

To reply to a specific message:

1. Swipe right on the message.

2. Type your response.

3. The original message will appear as a quote in your reply.

Filtering and Organizing Messages

Instagram allows users to filter messages for better organization:

- **Primary Inbox** – For important conversations.

- **General Inbox** – For less important messages.

- **Spam/Hidden Requests** – For messages that Instagram flags as suspicious.

You can also pin important conversations for quick access by swiping right on a chat and selecting **Pin**.

Reporting and Blocking Users

To report or block a user:

1. Open the chat.

2. Tap the **three-dot menu**.

3. Choose **Report** or **Block**.

Reporting is essential to maintain a safe and respectful environment on Instagram.

Conclusion

Instagram Direct Messaging is a versatile tool for personal connections, business engagement, and community building. By mastering its features, users can effectively communicate, build relationships, and enhance their Instagram experience.

3.4.3 Collaborating with Others on Instagram

Introduction to Instagram Collaborations

Collaboration is one of the most powerful strategies for growth and engagement on Instagram. By partnering with other users, influencers, or brands, you can reach a wider audience, boost credibility, and create engaging content that resonates with followers from multiple communities. Whether you're a content creator, business owner, or influencer, collaboration is key to building a dynamic and interactive Instagram presence.

In this section, we will explore various types of collaborations, strategies for finding the right partners, and best practices for making your Instagram collaborations successful.

Types of Instagram Collaborations

There are multiple ways to collaborate on Instagram, depending on your goals and target audience. Below are some of the most effective methods:

1. Co-Hosting Instagram Live Sessions

Instagram Live allows users to broadcast in real-time, and you can invite others to join as co-hosts. This is a great way to engage both audiences simultaneously and provide interactive, valuable content.

- **Benefits:** Increased visibility, audience engagement, and authenticity.
- **Best Practices:** Plan your session topics in advance, promote the event, and interact with viewers through Q&A sessions.

2. Collaborative Posts & Reels

Instagram allows users to tag collaborators in posts, making content visible to both audiences.

- **Benefits:** Higher engagement and credibility as your content reaches a broader audience.
- **Best Practices:** Ensure the content aligns with both brands' values, use compelling visuals, and craft engaging captions.

3. Takeovers

An Instagram takeover is when one user temporarily takes control of another user's account to engage with their audience.

- **Benefits:** Cross-promotion, audience growth, and fresh content.
- **Best Practices:** Set clear goals, outline expectations, and promote the takeover across both accounts.

4. Giveaways & Contests

Collaborating with other accounts to host giveaways can help increase followers and engagement.

- **Benefits:** Rapid audience growth, increased brand awareness, and enhanced engagement.
- **Best Practices:** Clearly define rules, choose valuable prizes, and use engagement-driven entry methods (e.g., tagging friends, following accounts, sharing posts).

5. Sponsored Content & Brand Partnerships

Brands often collaborate with influencers to create sponsored posts that promote products or services.

- **Benefits:** Monetization opportunities and increased trustworthiness.

- **Best Practices:** Ensure authenticity by choosing partnerships that align with your brand, disclose sponsorships transparently, and create high-quality content.

Finding the Right Collaboration Partners

To ensure a successful collaboration, it's essential to find partners that align with your brand and audience.

1. Identifying Potential Collaborators

- Look for users in your niche with similar engagement rates.

- Check mutual followers or influencer lists within your industry.

- Analyze potential partners' content quality and audience engagement.

2. Reaching Out to Collaborators

- **Personalized Direct Messages (DMs):** Introduce yourself, express admiration for their work, and propose a collaboration idea.

- **Email Outreach:** For professional partnerships, a formal email may be more appropriate.

- **Engaging with Their Content First:** Like, comment, and share their posts before reaching out.

3. Setting Clear Expectations

- Define objectives: follower growth, brand awareness, or sales.

- Establish content guidelines and responsibilities.

- Set a timeline and promotional plan.

Executing a Successful Instagram Collaboration

Once you have secured a collaboration partner, executing the campaign effectively is crucial.

1. Planning Your Content Strategy

- Decide on content formats (Reels, Stories, Carousel posts, Lives).
- Outline key messages and call-to-actions (CTAs).
- Create a posting schedule and agree on mutual promotion strategies.

2. Creating High-Quality Content

- Use professional images and videos.
- Ensure consistency in branding and aesthetics.
- Focus on storytelling to make content engaging.

3. Engaging Your Audience

- Encourage followers to participate by asking questions or using interactive stickers.
- Respond to comments and DMs.
- Use Instagram Insights to track engagement and adjust the strategy accordingly.

Measuring the Success of Collaborations

After the collaboration, it's essential to analyze performance and assess whether it met your goals.

1. Key Performance Metrics to Track

- **Engagement Rate:** Likes, comments, and shares.
- **Follower Growth:** New followers gained from the collaboration.
- **Reach & Impressions:** How many people saw the content.
- **Conversion Rate:** If applicable, track sales, sign-ups, or website visits.

2. Using Instagram Insights for Data Analysis

- Navigate to Instagram Insights to view post performance.
- Compare engagement metrics before and after the collaboration.
- Identify what worked well and what could be improved for future collaborations.

3. Gathering Feedback and Optimizing Future Collaborations

- Ask your audience for feedback through polls or direct messages.

- Discuss with your collaborator what aspects were successful.

- Adjust future strategies based on analytics and feedback.

Conclusion

Instagram collaborations can significantly boost your presence, engagement, and brand credibility. Whether through co-hosting live sessions, running giveaways, or creating sponsored content, strategic partnerships allow for organic growth and enhanced audience interaction. By selecting the right partners, planning effectively, and tracking performance, you can maximize the impact of Instagram collaborations and continuously refine your approach for future success.

CHAPTER III
Growing Your Audience

4.1 Understanding the Instagram Algorithm

4.1.1 How the Feed and Explore Page Work

Introduction

Instagram's Feed and Explore Page play a crucial role in content discovery and audience growth. Understanding how these features work will help you optimize your content strategy, reach more users, and increase engagement. This section will provide an in-depth look at how Instagram curates content for each user and how you can leverage this knowledge to enhance your visibility on the platform.

The Instagram Feed Algorithm

The Instagram Feed is the first thing users see when they open the app. It consists of posts from people they follow, sponsored ads, and suggested content. Instagram's algorithm determines the order in which these posts appear based on multiple factors, including relevance, user activity, and engagement levels.

Key Factors Influencing the Instagram Feed

1. **User Engagement History**

   o Instagram prioritizes posts from accounts a user frequently interacts with (e.g., likes, comments, shares, and direct messages).

   o If a user regularly engages with your content, your posts are more likely to appear at the top of their Feed.

2. **Post Popularity**

- o Posts with high engagement (likes, comments, shares, saves) within a short time after posting are favored by the algorithm.

- o More engagement signals that a post is valuable and relevant to a broader audience.

3. **Relevancy Score**

- o Instagram predicts how relevant a post is to a user based on past behavior.

- o If a user consistently interacts with posts about fitness, they are more likely to see fitness-related content in their Feed.

4. **Timeliness of Posts**

- o Recent posts are prioritized over older ones.

- o Posting when your audience is most active can help maximize visibility.

5. **Relationships and Interactions**

- o Posts from close connections, such as friends and family, are prioritized.

- o Frequent direct messaging and tagging also increase the likelihood of appearing in someone's Feed.

The Explore Page Algorithm

The Explore Page is where Instagram showcases content from accounts a user doesn't follow but may find interesting. It is tailored to individual preferences and designed to help users discover new content.

How Instagram Selects Content for the Explore Page

1. **User Activity and Interests**

- o The algorithm analyzes a user's past interactions to predict content preferences.

- o For example, if a user frequently watches travel videos, they will see more travel-related content on their Explore Page.

2. **Engagement on Similar Content**

- o Instagram identifies trending posts in specific categories and suggests them to users with similar interests.

- o High engagement on a post (likes, shares, saves) increases its chances of appearing on multiple Explore Pages.

3. **Content-Type Preferences**

- o If a user mostly engages with videos, their Explore Page will feature more video content.

- o Instagram adapts to content consumption habits, offering a personalized browsing experience.

4. **Trending Topics and Hashtags**

- o Popular trends and viral content often get featured on the Explore Page.

- o Using trending hashtags and participating in viral challenges can improve your chances of being discovered.

Strategies to Optimize Your Content for the Feed and Explore Page

Optimizing for the Feed

1. **Post at Peak Times**

- o Analyze Instagram Insights to determine when your audience is most active.

- o Schedule posts accordingly to maximize engagement.

2. **Encourage Engagement**

- o Ask questions in captions to spark conversations.

- o Use calls-to-action (CTAs) such as "Double-tap if you agree" or "Tag a friend who needs to see this!"

3. **Consistent and High-Quality Content**

- o Post visually appealing images and videos.

- o Maintain a consistent aesthetic to build brand recognition.

4. **Leverage Instagram Stories and Reels**

   - Stories keep you at the top of followers' Feeds.

   - Reels have a high chance of reaching new audiences through the Explore Page.

Optimizing for the Explore Page

1. **Use Relevant Hashtags and Keywords**

   - Research trending and niche-specific hashtags.

   - Include keywords in captions to enhance discoverability.

2. **Engage with Similar Accounts**

   - Like, comment, and share posts within your niche to increase exposure.

   - Engaging with trending content boosts visibility.

3. **Create Shareable Content**

   - Content that evokes emotions (funny, inspirational, relatable) is more likely to be shared.

   - The more shares a post gets, the higher its chances of appearing on the Explore Page.

4. **Post Consistently and Experiment with Content Formats**

   - Regular posting signals activity and reliability to Instagram's algorithm.

   - Experiment with carousels, videos, and reels to see what resonates best with your audience.

Conclusion

Understanding how Instagram's Feed and Explore Page work is key to growing your audience. By optimizing your content strategy based on engagement, relevance, and timing, you can increase your visibility and reach a wider audience. Stay consistent, experiment with different strategies, and track your performance using Instagram Insights to refine your approach.

4.1.2 Best Times to Post for Maximum Engagement

Instagram is a dynamic platform where engagement levels fluctuate throughout the day. Knowing the best times to post can significantly impact how many people see and interact with your content. While there is no universal "perfect" time that works for everyone, research and data-driven insights can help you determine the optimal posting schedule for your audience.

Understanding Audience Behavior

One of the first steps in determining the best times to post is understanding your audience's habits. Instagram users are active at different times based on their demographics, location, and lifestyle. Some key factors to consider include:

- **Time zones:** If your audience is spread across multiple time zones, you may need to adjust your posting schedule accordingly.

- **Age group:** Teenagers and young adults might be more active in the late afternoon and evenings, while professionals may check Instagram during lunch breaks or early mornings.

- **Daily routines:** Consider when your target audience is likely to scroll through Instagram. For example, many people check social media during their morning commute, lunch break, or before bed.

General Best Times to Post on Instagram

Multiple studies from social media analytics companies have identified trends in Instagram engagement. While results may vary based on niche and audience, some general guidelines include:

- **Best Days to Post:** Tuesday, Wednesday, and Thursday tend to have the highest engagement rates.

- **Best Times to Post:** Generally, the following time slots yield good engagement:

  - **Early morning (6 AM - 8 AM):** Many users check Instagram as soon as they wake up.

  - **Lunch break (11 AM - 1 PM):** Engagement spikes as people scroll through Instagram during breaks.

- **Evening (6 PM - 9 PM):** Users are winding down after work or school and spending more time on social media.

- **Late night (10 PM - 12 AM):** Some users, particularly younger audiences, engage with content before going to bed.

Industry-Specific Posting Times

Different industries and content types may perform better at different times. Below are recommended posting times based on industry:

- **Retail & E-commerce:** Best engagement occurs on weekdays between **12 PM - 3 PM** and **7 PM - 9 PM** when users are browsing for products.

- **Fitness & Wellness:** Early mornings (**6 AM - 9 AM**) work best as users check Instagram before workouts.

- **Food & Beverage:** Midday (**12 PM - 2 PM**) and evenings (**6 PM - 8 PM**) see high engagement as people plan meals.

- **Technology & Business:** Mornings (**7 AM - 10 AM**) and lunchtime (**12 PM - 1 PM**) tend to have the best results as professionals check their phones.

- **Entertainment & Media:** Evenings and weekends (**6 PM - 10 PM**) receive the most engagement when users have free time.

Using Instagram Insights to Find Your Best Times

Instagram provides built-in analytics for business and creator accounts that can help you determine when your audience is most active. To access these insights:

1. Open the **Instagram app** and go to your **profile**.

2. Tap on **Insights**.

3. Select **Total Followers** to see audience demographics, including the most active times and days.

4. Analyze the engagement patterns and adjust your posting schedule accordingly.

By leveraging Instagram Insights, you can fine-tune your strategy and post at times that yield the highest engagement.

Scheduling and Automating Your Posts

Once you determine the best times to post, you can use scheduling tools to ensure consistency. Some popular tools include:

- **Meta Business Suite:** Instagram's official scheduling tool.

- **Later:** A user-friendly tool for visual content planning.

- **Hootsuite:** Ideal for managing multiple social media accounts.

- **Buffer:** A simple and efficient scheduling platform.

These tools allow you to plan and automate posts, ensuring you never miss an optimal posting time.

Testing and Adapting Your Posting Strategy

Since engagement trends can change, it's essential to test different posting times and analyze results. Here are some tips:

- **A/B testing:** Post the same type of content at different times and compare engagement rates.

- **Track engagement metrics:** Pay attention to likes, comments, shares, and saves.

- **Adjust based on performance:** If certain times show better results, shift your posting schedule accordingly.

Conclusion

The best times to post on Instagram vary based on your audience, industry, and content strategy. By analyzing your followers' behavior, leveraging Instagram Insights, and using scheduling tools, you can maximize engagement and grow your audience effectively. Regularly reviewing and adapting your strategy will ensure continued success on the platform.

4.1.3 How to Increase Visibility

Instagram is a highly competitive platform with millions of posts being shared every day. To stand out and increase your visibility, you need to implement effective strategies that optimize your content for the Instagram algorithm, engage with your audience, and leverage platform features. This section explores key techniques to enhance your reach and maximize your presence on Instagram.

1. Optimize Your Content for the Algorithm

The Instagram algorithm prioritizes content based on engagement, relevance, and timeliness. To increase visibility, you must create content that resonates with your audience and encourages interactions.

- **Post High-Quality Content:** Instagram is a visual platform, so make sure your images and videos are high-resolution, well-edited, and aesthetically appealing.

- **Use Engaging Captions:** Write compelling captions that prompt users to comment, share, or save your posts. Questions, storytelling, and calls-to-action (CTAs) work well.

- **Leverage Carousels:** Posts with multiple images or videos tend to get more engagement, which signals to the algorithm that your content is valuable.

- **Utilize Instagram's Latest Features:** The algorithm favors content that incorporates new platform features like Reels, interactive stickers in Stories, and collaborative posts.

2. Master the Art of Hashtags and Geotags

Hashtags and geotags are essential tools for increasing the discoverability of your posts.

- **Use Relevant Hashtags:** Research and use a mix of trending, niche, and branded hashtags to expand your reach. Instagram allows up to 30 hashtags per post, but the sweet spot is usually between 5-15.

- **Avoid Banned or Overused Hashtags:** Some hashtags are flagged by Instagram and using them may reduce your visibility. Always check before using a hashtag.

- **Utilize Geotags:** Adding a location to your post can make it more discoverable, especially for local audiences and businesses.

3. Post at the Right Time

Timing plays a crucial role in visibility. Posting when your audience is most active increases engagement and signals to the algorithm that your content is relevant.

- **Analyze Instagram Insights:** Use Instagram analytics to determine when your followers are most active.

- **Experiment with Posting Times:** Test different posting times and track engagement to find what works best for your audience.

- **Be Consistent:** Posting consistently helps maintain audience interest and improves your chances of appearing on the Explore Page.

4. Engage with Your Audience

Engagement is a two-way street. The more you interact with your audience, the higher your chances of being favored by the algorithm.

- **Respond to Comments and Messages:** Replying to comments and DMs fosters a sense of community and encourages more interactions.

- **Encourage Conversations:** Ask questions in your captions or create interactive Stories using polls, quizzes, and Q&A stickers.

- **Engage with Other Accounts:** Like, comment, and share content from similar or complementary accounts to build relationships and expand your reach.

5. Utilize Instagram Stories and Reels

Instagram Stories and Reels are powerful tools for increasing visibility and keeping your audience engaged.

- **Post Stories Regularly:** Stories appear at the top of the feed and can keep your audience engaged throughout the day.

- **Use Interactive Features:** Polls, quizzes, countdowns, and question stickers increase engagement and encourage interactions.

- **Create Reels:** Reels are currently favored by the algorithm and have a high chance of appearing on the Explore Page. Use trending sounds, transitions, and effects to boost your reach.

6. Leverage Instagram Collaborations and Cross-Promotion

Partnering with other users or brands can significantly expand your visibility.

- **Use Instagram Collabs:** This feature allows two accounts to co-author a post or Reel, doubling the reach.

- **Cross-Promote on Other Platforms:** Share your Instagram content on Facebook, Twitter, TikTok, and Pinterest to attract new followers.

- **Host Giveaways and Contests:** Encourage users to tag friends and share your content as part of the contest mechanics to boost visibility.

7. Get Featured on the Explore Page

The Explore Page is where users discover new content tailored to their interests. Getting featured here can significantly increase your visibility.

- **Create Shareable Content:** The more people share, save, and engage with your post, the higher the chances of appearing on the Explore Page.

- **Use Trending Audio and Effects:** Instagram promotes content that aligns with current trends.

- **Engage with Niche Communities:** Interacting with niche-specific content increases your chances of being recommended to similar users.

8. Monitor and Adjust Your Strategy

Increasing visibility on Instagram requires continuous monitoring and optimization.

- **Use Instagram Insights:** Track your post performance, audience demographics, and engagement metrics.

- **Adjust Based on Data:** If certain content types perform better, focus on creating more of that.

- **Stay Updated on Algorithm Changes:** Instagram frequently updates its algorithm, so stay informed and adapt accordingly.

By implementing these strategies consistently, you can increase your visibility, grow your audience, and establish a strong presence on Instagram. The key is to stay engaged, experiment with different approaches, and continuously refine your content strategy based on data and trends.

4.2 Building a Strong Follower Base

4.2.1 Finding and Attracting the Right Audience

Understanding Your Ideal Audience

Before you start growing your Instagram following, it's crucial to identify who your ideal audience is. Having a clear understanding of your target audience will help you create content that resonates with them, ensuring better engagement and long-term loyalty. Here are some key questions to consider:

- Who are your potential followers? (Age, gender, interests, location, etc.)

- What type of content do they consume on Instagram?

- What problems or needs do they have that your content can solve?

- When are they most active on Instagram?

Defining these aspects will help you tailor your content, captions, and engagement strategies to attract the right people to your profile.

Optimizing Your Profile for the Right Audience

Your Instagram profile is the first impression new visitors get when they land on your page. A well-optimized profile encourages users to follow you. Here's how to optimize it effectively:

1. Profile Picture and Username

- Choose a recognizable profile picture, such as your brand logo or a professional headshot.

- Keep your username simple and easy to remember.

2. Bio and Description

- Write a compelling bio that clearly states who you are and what value you provide.

- Use keywords related to your niche to improve discoverability.

- Add a call-to-action (CTA), such as "Follow for daily marketing tips" or "Click the link below for exclusive content."

3. Link in Bio

- Use the bio link wisely to direct followers to your website, blog, online store, or latest content.
- Consider using tools like Linktree to provide multiple link options.

Creating Content That Appeals to Your Target Audience

Content is the backbone of audience growth. If your content isn't relevant, engaging, and valuable to your target audience, they won't follow or interact with your account. Here's how to craft content that attracts the right followers:

1. Research Audience Preferences

- Use Instagram Insights to analyze the demographics and behaviors of your current audience.
- Observe successful competitors and influencers in your niche to see what works for them.
- Conduct polls and ask your followers what type of content they enjoy.

2. Create High-Quality Visual Content

- Post high-resolution photos and well-edited videos to maintain a professional look.
- Stick to a consistent theme and color scheme to establish a strong brand identity.

3. Post Engaging Captions

- Use storytelling techniques to make your captions more engaging.
- Ask questions and encourage audience interaction.
- Use emojis strategically to add personality.

4. Leverage Instagram Reels and Stories

- Short-form videos (Reels) often reach a larger audience and gain higher engagement.
- Use Stories to connect with followers in a more casual and interactive way.

Using Hashtags and Geotags Strategically

Hashtags and geotags improve the discoverability of your content and help attract relevant audiences. Here's how to use them effectively:

1. Choosing the Right Hashtags

- Use a mix of popular, niche, and branded hashtags.
- Research trending hashtags in your industry.
- Avoid banned or overly generic hashtags.

2. Using Geotags for Local Engagement

- Tag locations relevant to your content to attract a local audience.
- Engage with users who have posted content in the same location.

Engaging with Your Target Audience

Growth isn't just about posting content—it's about building relationships. Here's how to actively engage with the right people:

1. Comment and Interact on Other Profiles

- Leave thoughtful comments on posts by influencers and users in your niche.
- Engage with people who comment on your competitors' posts.

2. Respond to Comments and DMs

- Show appreciation by responding to followers' comments and messages.
- Build relationships through meaningful conversations.

3. Join and Contribute to Instagram Communities

- Participate in Instagram groups and communities related to your niche.
- Engage in trending discussions and contribute valuable insights.

Collaborating with Others to Reach the Right Audience

Networking and collaborations can help you attract the right followers. Here's how:

1. Partner with Influencers

- Collaborate with influencers whose followers align with your target audience.
- Opt for micro-influencers with high engagement rates if you have a smaller budget.

2. Participate in Giveaways and Contests

- Team up with brands or creators for a joint giveaway.
- Ensure that the giveaway attracts an audience genuinely interested in your content.

3. Cross-Promote on Other Platforms

- Promote your Instagram profile on your website, YouTube, TikTok, or other social media platforms.
- Leverage email marketing to drive existing customers to your Instagram.

Tracking Progress and Adjusting Your Strategy

To ensure you are attracting and retaining the right audience, consistently analyze your Instagram performance:

- Use Instagram Insights to track follower demographics and engagement.
- Identify what types of content generate the most interactions.
- Continuously refine your strategy based on data and feedback.

Conclusion

Finding and attracting the right audience on Instagram requires a combination of clear audience understanding, profile optimization, strategic content creation, active engagement, and smart collaborations. By implementing these strategies, you can grow a highly engaged following that aligns with your brand and goals.

4.2.2 Networking with Influencers and Brands

Introduction

Building relationships with influencers and brands is a crucial strategy for growing your audience on Instagram. Effective networking can help increase your reach, credibility, and engagement, opening doors to new collaborations, sponsorships, and long-term partnerships. Whether you are an aspiring influencer, a content creator, or a business owner, understanding how to connect with the right people on Instagram can significantly impact your growth.

This section will guide you through the best practices for networking with influencers and brands, covering how to find the right connections, approach potential partners, and build lasting relationships that benefit all parties involved.

1. Understanding the Power of Networking on Instagram

Networking on Instagram is more than just following people or engaging with their posts—it's about establishing meaningful connections that lead to mutual growth. Successful networking can:

- Expand your audience by exposing your content to a larger group.

- Increase engagement through collaborations and shoutouts.

- Enhance credibility by associating with reputable influencers or brands.

- Open opportunities for sponsorships and brand deals.

By leveraging these connections, you can elevate your Instagram presence and gain access to new markets and opportunities.

2. Finding the Right Influencers and Brands

2.1 Identifying the Right Influencers

Not all influencers will align with your brand or content, so it's essential to find those who share your niche, values, and audience. Here's how to identify the right influencers:

- **Relevance:** Look for influencers who create content that aligns with your industry or brand.

- **Engagement Rate:** High engagement is more valuable than a high follower count. Check the number of likes, comments, and shares relative to their followers.

- **Authenticity:** Ensure the influencer has a genuine connection with their audience and does not rely on fake engagement.

- **Content Quality:** Look at the consistency, aesthetic, and professionalism of their posts.

- **Audience Demographics:** Make sure their followers match your target market.

You can find influencers by:

- Exploring Instagram's "Suggested for You" feature.

- Searching relevant hashtags in your niche.

- Using influencer marketing platforms like Upfluence, Heepsy, or AspireIQ.

- Checking your competitors' collaborations.

2.2 Finding Brands to Collaborate With

If you're an influencer or content creator, brands can help you grow through sponsorships and collaborations. To find potential brand partners:

- Identify brands that align with your niche and personal values.

- Research brands that are already working with influencers in your space.

- Follow and engage with brands to get on their radar.

- Use influencer-brand matching platforms like Tribe, FameBit, or Collabstr.

- Look for brand partnership announcements and callouts in industry forums.

3. How to Approach Influencers and Brands

3.1 Engaging Before Reaching Out

Before sending a direct message (DM) or email, it's best to interact with influencers and brands organically. Here's how:

- **Like and comment** on their posts with thoughtful responses.

- **Share their content** in your stories with a mention.

- **Reply to their stories** with relevant feedback or questions.

- **Tag them in relevant posts** (without spamming) to show appreciation.

This warm-up process increases the chances of them recognizing you when you eventually reach out.

3.2 Crafting a Personalized Outreach Message

Once you have engaged with an influencer or brand, the next step is to reach out directly. A well-crafted message should be:

- **Personalized:** Mention specific things you admire about their content or brand.

- **Concise:** Get to the point without a lengthy introduction.

- **Value-driven:** Highlight what's in it for them.

- **Clear Call to Action:** Suggest a simple next step.

Example of a DM to an influencer:

"Hey [Influencer's Name], I love your content on [specific topic]—your recent post about [specific post] really resonated with me! I'd love to collaborate on [collaboration idea]. I think our audiences would really enjoy it. Let me know if you're interested!"

Example of an email to a brand:

"Subject: Collaboration Opportunity with [Your Name]

Hi [Brand Representative's Name],

I'm [Your Name], a [your niche] content creator passionate about [specific topic]. I've been following your brand for a while, and I love [specific aspect of the brand].

I'd love to explore a collaboration where I showcase your products to my engaged audience of [mention your audience size and engagement]. I have some creative ideas that could benefit both of us. Would you be open to discussing this?

Looking forward to your thoughts!

Best, [Your Name]"

4. Building Long-Term Relationships

Networking is not just about one-time collaborations but about fostering lasting relationships. Here's how to maintain connections:

- **Stay engaged** by consistently interacting with their content.

- **Show appreciation** by thanking them for any collaboration.

- **Provide value** by sharing useful insights or new opportunities.

- **Follow up** periodically to check in and propose new ideas.

Long-term partnerships often lead to bigger opportunities such as brand ambassadorships, ongoing sponsorships, and exclusive collaborations.

Conclusion

Networking with influencers and brands on Instagram requires a strategic and thoughtful approach. By identifying the right partners, engaging authentically, reaching out effectively, and nurturing long-term relationships, you can leverage these connections to grow your audience and open new opportunities.

4.2.3 Avoiding Fake Followers and Bots

Introduction

Building a genuine follower base on Instagram is crucial for long-term success, whether you are an influencer, brand, or business. However, the temptation to gain followers quickly can lead people to purchase fake followers or engage with bots. While this may seem like an easy way to boost numbers, it comes with significant drawbacks, including reduced engagement, algorithm penalties, and credibility loss. In this section, we will explore how to identify fake followers, understand their negative impact, and adopt best practices to maintain an authentic and engaged audience.

The Risks of Fake Followers and Bots

1. Low Engagement Rate

Fake followers are not real people, which means they will not interact with your content. Instagram's algorithm prioritizes engagement (likes, comments, shares, and saves) to determine the reach of your posts. If you have a high follower count but a low engagement rate, Instagram may flag your account as having inauthentic activity, which can reduce your content's visibility.

2. Algorithm Penalties

Instagram continuously updates its algorithm to detect and penalize inauthentic engagement. Accounts with a high percentage of fake followers may experience:

- A significant drop in organic reach.

- Lower ranking on the Explore page.

- Decreased visibility in hashtags.

- Shadowbanning, where posts are hidden from non-followers.

3. Loss of Credibility

Authenticity is key to building trust with your audience. If people discover that you have inflated your follower count artificially, your credibility may suffer. Brands, collaborators, and potential sponsors often check engagement metrics, and a low engagement-to-follower ratio can indicate purchased followers.

4. Risk of Account Suspension

Instagram actively removes fake accounts and may temporarily or permanently suspend accounts that repeatedly violate its policies. If your account is linked to fraudulent activities, you may lose your hard-earned content and audience.

How to Identify Fake Followers and Bots

1. Check Engagement Metrics

A healthy Instagram account should have an engagement rate between 1% and 5%. If you notice thousands of followers but only a handful of likes or comments on posts, it could indicate fake followers.

2. Analyze Followers' Profiles

Fake accounts often share common traits:

- No profile picture or a generic stock image.

- Few or no posts.

- A username with random characters or numbers (e.g., user12345).
- Following thousands of accounts but having very few followers themselves.

3. Monitor Comments for Spam

Fake accounts and bots often leave generic or irrelevant comments such as:

- "Nice post!"
- "DM us for a collab!"
- Emojis with no meaningful interaction.

If you notice a large number of such comments, your account may be attracting bot activity.

4. Look for Sudden Follower Spikes

A rapid increase in followers within a short period, without a viral post or a strong marketing campaign, is a red flag. You can use tools like Social Blade or Instagram Insights to track follower growth trends.

How to Remove Fake Followers

1. Manually Remove Suspicious Accounts

Go to your followers list and remove any accounts that appear fake. This process can be time-consuming but is essential for maintaining a genuine audience.

2. Use Third-Party Tools

Platforms like HypeAuditor, FakeCheck, or IG Audit can help identify fake followers and suggest removal strategies.

3. Block and Report Bots

If you notice a bot account following you, report it to Instagram and block it to prevent further interactions.

4. Avoid Engagement Pods

Engagement pods, where groups of people artificially boost each other's posts, may seem beneficial but can result in Instagram detecting and penalizing inauthentic activity.

Building an Organic and Engaged Audience

1. Create High-Quality Content

Focus on producing valuable, visually appealing, and engaging content that resonates with your audience. Use professional photography, storytelling, and interactive elements like polls and Q&A sessions.

2. Engage Authentically

Reply to comments, ask questions in captions, and interact with followers via Instagram Stories and direct messages.

3. Collaborate with Real People

Partner with authentic influencers and brands to reach a broader audience. Avoid collaborations with individuals who use fake followers.

4. Use Hashtags Strategically

Research and use relevant hashtags to increase discoverability. Avoid banned or overly generic hashtags that may attract bots.

5. Post Consistently

Maintain a consistent posting schedule to keep your audience engaged. Instagram's algorithm favors accounts that post regularly and interact with their followers.

6. Leverage Instagram Insights

Use Instagram's built-in analytics to monitor engagement metrics and adjust your strategy based on real audience behavior.

Conclusion

Avoiding fake followers and bots is essential for sustainable growth on Instagram. While artificially inflating numbers may provide short-term vanity metrics, it ultimately harms your credibility, engagement, and potential for real success. By focusing on authentic interactions, high-quality content, and strategic engagement, you can build a loyal and valuable audience that genuinely supports your brand or personal profile. Stay patient, be consistent, and watch your real Instagram influence grow.

4.3 Mastering Hashtags and Geotags

4.3.1 Finding the Best Hashtags for Your Niche

105,487 likes

shouxin13141 It's time for some cuteness overload, four little line-drawn cats and dogs are waiting for you! 🐾 #shouxinsketch #petart #animalart #illustrationartists #dog #lovepuppies #cat #pet #sketch #sketchdaily

View all 135 comments

Add a comment...

Introduction to Hashtags on Instagram

Hashtags play a crucial role in content discovery on Instagram. They help categorize content, increase reach, and connect users with similar interests. When used strategically, hashtags can significantly enhance your engagement and visibility. However, simply using popular hashtags is not enough; you need to find the right ones that align with your niche.

Why Hashtags Matter for Your Niche

Instagram's algorithm prioritizes content that is relevant to users' interests. By using targeted hashtags, you ensure that your posts appear in front of the right audience. Hashtags can help you:

- Increase the discoverability of your content
- Connect with potential followers interested in your niche
- Improve engagement rates
- Boost your chances of being featured on the Explore page

Types of Hashtags to Consider

To maximize your hashtag strategy, you should incorporate different types of hashtags:

1. **Branded Hashtags**

   o These are unique hashtags specific to your brand, business, or personal identity.

   o Example: #NikeRunClub for Nike's running community.

2. **Industry-Specific Hashtags**

   o These relate to the general industry you are in.

   o Example: #PhotographyTips for photographers.

3. **Niche-Specific Hashtags**

   o These target a smaller, more engaged community within your industry.

   o Example: #MinimalistPhotography for minimalism-focused photographers.

4. **Community Hashtags**

   o Used by groups sharing a common interest, helping you tap into engaged communities.

   o Example: #WritersOfInstagram for writers.

5. **Event Hashtags**

   o Used for events, conferences, or holidays.

   o Example: #Coachella2025 for the Coachella festival.

6. **Location-Based Hashtags**

   o Useful for businesses and influencers who want to target audiences in specific locations.

   o Example: #NYCFoodie for food lovers in New York City.

How to Find the Best Hashtags for Your Niche

Finding the best hashtags requires research and experimentation. Here's how you can discover the most effective hashtags for your niche:

1. Research Your Competitors

Look at what hashtags industry leaders and competitors are using. Take note of:

- The number of likes and comments on posts using these hashtags.

- The variety of hashtags used.

- Which hashtags appear frequently in your niche.

2. Use Instagram's Search Feature

Instagram allows you to search for hashtags and see how many posts use them. To find niche-specific hashtags:

- Go to the Instagram search bar.

- Type a keyword relevant to your niche.

- Select the 'Tags' tab to see related hashtags and their post counts.

3. Explore the Related Hashtags Feature

When you search for a hashtag, Instagram suggests related hashtags. These can provide valuable insights into what other hashtags might work well for your content.

4. Use Hashtag Research Tools

There are several online tools available that help analyze and generate relevant hashtags, such as:

- **Hashtagify** – Provides insights into trending hashtags and their popularity.

- **RiteTag** – Suggests hashtags based on image and text analysis.

- **All Hashtag** – Generates and analyzes hashtag performance.

5. Check Engagement Metrics

Using hashtags with millions of posts might not always be the best strategy. Instead, consider:

- **High-volume hashtags (500K+ posts)** – Great for general exposure but high competition.

- **Medium-volume hashtags (50K – 500K posts)** – Balanced exposure with better engagement opportunities.

- **Low-volume hashtags (under 50K posts)** – Niche-specific, ideal for targeting a dedicated audience.

How to Implement Hashtags Effectively

Once you've identified the best hashtags, you need to use them strategically:

1. Mix Popular and Niche Hashtags

A good mix of high-volume and niche-specific hashtags ensures visibility while maintaining engagement.

2. Use Hashtags in the Right Places

- **In the caption** – Makes hashtags visible and easily clickable.

- **In the first comment** – Keeps captions clean while still ensuring discoverability.

3. Limit the Number of Hashtags

Instagram allows up to 30 hashtags per post, but using all of them can appear spammy. A recommended range is:

- 5-10 targeted hashtags for maximum effectiveness.

4. Test and Adjust Your Hashtags

Monitor which hashtags drive the most engagement and adjust accordingly. Keep a rotating list to avoid overuse and shadowbanning risks.

Common Mistakes to Avoid

- **Using only generic hashtags** (e.g., #love, #instagood) – They are too broad and highly competitive.

- **Not changing hashtags regularly** – Instagram may flag repetitive use as spam.

- **Using banned or restricted hashtags** – Always check if a hashtag is active before using it.

- **Ignoring analytics** – Always track the performance of hashtags to optimize your strategy.

Conclusion

Hashtags are a powerful tool when used strategically. By focusing on niche-specific hashtags and consistently analyzing performance, you can increase engagement and grow your Instagram presence. Experiment with different combinations and refine your approach to maximize your success on the platform.

4.3.2 Using Location Tags for Local Engagement

Introduction

Instagram's location tagging feature is a powerful tool for increasing engagement, attracting new followers, and enhancing visibility within specific geographic areas. Whether you are a business looking to attract local customers, an influencer wanting to connect with audiences in a particular region, or a traveler documenting experiences, using location tags effectively can significantly boost your reach. This chapter will explore the benefits of location tags, best practices for using them, and strategies to maximize engagement.

The Power of Location Tags

Location tags, also known as geotags, allow users to attach a specific place to their posts, stories, and reels. When a post is tagged with a location, it becomes discoverable in the location's dedicated feed, allowing other users interested in that area to find and interact with it. This feature is particularly useful for:

- **Businesses**: Promoting a physical store, event, or pop-up shop.
- **Influencers**: Targeting audiences from a specific city or region.
- **Tourism and Hospitality**: Showcasing destinations, hotels, and attractions.
- **Local Communities**: Encouraging interactions among residents and visitors.

How Location Tags Work

Instagram aggregates posts tagged with the same location into a location-based feed. Users searching for that location or clicking on the tag in someone else's post will see all public content associated with that place. This increases exposure and can drive engagement from people interested in that specific area.

Types of Location Tags on Instagram

1. **City or General Area Tags**: Broad locations such as "New York City" or "Paris, France."
2. **Specific Business or Venue Tags**: Restaurants, cafes, hotels, gyms, and stores.
3. **Landmarks and Attractions**: Museums, parks, stadiums, and popular sites.
4. **Neighborhood or District Tags**: Soho, Brooklyn, or Shoreditch.

Best Practices for Using Location Tags

To maximize engagement, simply adding a location tag is not enough. You need a strategic approach. Below are key practices:

1. Choose the Right Location

- If you are posting for business purposes, tag your store, office, or event venue.

- If you are an influencer or traveler, use tags relevant to your content to attract like-minded audiences.

- Experiment with broad and niche locations. A city tag may reach more people, but a specific business or landmark can target a niche audience.

2. Use Location Tags in Stories and Reels

- Instagram Stories and Reels with location tags often get higher visibility because they appear in location-based stories.

- Engage with users who view your story by responding to comments or questions about the location.

3. Engage with Other Users at the Same Location

- Browse posts under the same location tag and engage with other users by liking and commenting.

- Follow local influencers and businesses that use the same location tag.

4. Combine Location Tags with Relevant Hashtags

- A post with both a location tag and targeted hashtags (e.g., #NYCFoodie, #MiamiBeach) increases discoverability.

- Mix general and niche hashtags to reach different audience segments.

5. Encourage User-Generated Content

- If you run a business, encourage customers to tag your location in their posts.

- Repost tagged content to your stories to increase visibility and build community engagement.

6. Use Geotags for Events and Promotions

- Hosting an event? Ask attendees to tag the event location.

- Run a contest where users must post with a specific location tag to enter.

Advanced Strategies for Local Engagement

To take your location tagging strategy to the next level, consider these advanced techniques:

1. Create a Custom Location Tag

Businesses and influencers can create a custom location on Instagram (via Facebook's Place Creation feature) for branding and community building.

2. Monitor Analytics for Location Tags

Instagram Insights provides data on which locations generate the most engagement. Use this data to refine your strategy.

3. Collaborate with Local Influencers

Partner with influencers in a specific area to increase reach. Their followers are likely to engage with content tagged in the same location.

4. Utilize Instagram Ads with Geotargeting

Instagram Ads allow you to target audiences by location. Combine this with organic location tagging for maximum impact.

5. Participate in Local Trends and Challenges

Pay attention to trending locations and participate in location-based challenges or events.

Conclusion

Using location tags strategically can help grow your audience, increase engagement, and connect with local communities. Whether you are an individual looking to boost your reach or a business aiming to attract customers, leveraging location tags effectively is a game-changer. By following best practices and employing advanced strategies, you can maximize your presence on Instagram and build a more engaged audience.

4.3.3 Common Mistakes to Avoid

Hashtags and geotags are powerful tools for increasing visibility on Instagram, but many users fail to use them effectively. Misusing these features can lead to lower engagement, a decline in follower growth, or even penalties from Instagram. Here are some of the most common mistakes users make when using hashtags and geotags, along with best practices to avoid them.

1. Using Irrelevant Hashtags

One of the biggest mistakes is using hashtags that are not related to your content. Some users think that adding popular or trending hashtags, even if unrelated, will help their post gain traction. However, this can backfire because:

- It attracts the wrong audience who will not engage with your content.
- Your post may be marked as spam by Instagram's algorithm.
- Users may report your content as irrelevant, decreasing your reach.

How to Avoid It:

- Research and choose hashtags that are directly relevant to your post and niche.
- Use Instagram's search function to find popular and niche-specific hashtags.
- Monitor which hashtags bring the best engagement and refine your strategy accordingly.

2. Overloading Posts with Hashtags

Instagram allows up to 30 hashtags per post, but using all 30 without a strategy can look spammy. Overloading hashtags can make your caption look cluttered and reduce readability.

How to Avoid It:

- Use a mix of broad and niche hashtags (5–15 well-researched hashtags per post is ideal).
- Place hashtags in a comment instead of the caption to maintain a clean look.
- Prioritize quality over quantity by selecting only the most relevant hashtags.

3. Using Banned or Overused Hashtags

Instagram occasionally bans or restricts certain hashtags due to misuse, spam, or inappropriate content. Using these hashtags can reduce your visibility or even cause your account to be shadowbanned.

How to Avoid It:

- Check if a hashtag is banned by searching for it on Instagram. If posts are hidden or the hashtag has no recent activity, avoid using it.

- Avoid generic or commonly spammed hashtags like #followforfollow or #like4like.

- Regularly update your hashtag list to ensure compliance with Instagram's policies.

4. Not Varying Hashtag Usage

Using the same set of hashtags in every post can lead to Instagram flagging your account as spammy. This can negatively impact your reach and engagement.

How to Avoid It:

- Rotate different sets of hashtags for different types of content.

- Create hashtag lists categorized by content themes and alternate between them.

- Test different hashtags to see which ones perform best for your content.

5. Using Highly Competitive Hashtags Only

Popular hashtags like #love, #instagood, or #fashion have millions of posts, making it difficult for your content to stand out. Posts under these hashtags get buried quickly due to high competition.

How to Avoid It:

- Use a combination of high-volume and low-competition hashtags.

- Target niche-specific hashtags that have between 10K–500K posts for better discoverability.

- Mix hashtags with different levels of engagement potential.

6. Not Using Location Tags in Posts and Stories

Geotags help local audiences find your content, yet many users overlook them. Not tagging a location can reduce your chances of being discovered by users searching for content in a specific area.

How to Avoid It:

- Always add location tags for posts, especially if they feature local businesses, landmarks, or events.
- Use geotags in Instagram Stories to increase visibility.
- Experiment with different location tags to see which attract more engagement.

7. Relying Solely on Hashtags for Growth

While hashtags help with discovery, they should not be your only strategy for growth. Many users expect instant follower growth just by adding hashtags but fail to engage with their audience.

How to Avoid It:

- Combine hashtags with strong content, engaging captions, and active interactions.
- Engage with other posts using the same hashtags by liking and commenting.
- Focus on creating valuable content that naturally attracts engagement.

8. Ignoring Instagram Insights

Not tracking your hashtag performance can lead to ineffective strategies. Instagram Insights provides data on which hashtags are driving the most engagement.

How to Avoid It:

- Regularly check Instagram Insights to see which hashtags generate the most impressions.
- Remove underperforming hashtags from your strategy.
- Continuously experiment with new hashtags to optimize results.

9. Using Too Many Generic Hashtags

Generic hashtags like #photooftheday or #happy are often too broad and do not target a specific audience. This makes it harder for your content to reach the right people.

How to Avoid It:

- Use industry-specific and branded hashtags to attract a relevant audience.

- Mix trending hashtags with niche hashtags for better visibility.

- Research competitors and influencers to see which hashtags work best in your industry.

10. Forgetting to Refresh Hashtag Strategies

Trends on Instagram change frequently, and hashtags that worked months ago may no longer be effective. Failing to update your hashtag strategy can lead to stagnation in growth.

How to Avoid It:

- Stay updated on industry trends and adjust your hashtags accordingly.

- Test new hashtags regularly and track their performance.

- Remove outdated hashtags that no longer bring engagement.

Final Thoughts

Avoiding these common mistakes can significantly improve your Instagram reach and engagement. Hashtags and geotags should be used strategically to attract the right audience, boost post visibility, and enhance brand recognition. By refining your hashtag and geotag strategy, you can maximize the effectiveness of your Instagram marketing efforts and grow your account organically.

CHAPTER IV
Advanced Instagram Strategies

5.1 Instagram for Business and Branding

5.1.1 Switching to a Business or Creator Account

Instagram offers three types of accounts: **Personal, Business, and Creator**. While the Personal account is suitable for casual users, Business and Creator accounts provide additional tools for branding, marketing, and audience engagement. If you want to establish a brand presence, promote products, or leverage Instagram's analytical tools, switching to a Business or Creator account is a strategic move.

Understanding the Differences Between Business and Creator Accounts

Before switching, it's important to understand the key distinctions between Business and Creator accounts:

Feature	Business Account	Creator Account
Instagram Insights	Yes	Yes
Contact Buttons	Yes	Yes
Instagram Shopping	Yes	No
Access to Ads	Yes	Yes

Feature	Business Account	Creator Account
Category Labeling	Yes	Yes
Saved Replies	Yes	No
Music Library	Limited	Full Access
Monetization Tools	No	Yes
Primary Audience	Businesses, Brands	Influencers, Content Creators

- **Business Account**: Best suited for companies, retailers, service providers, and brands aiming to use Instagram for sales, customer engagement, and advertising.
- **Creator Account**: Designed for influencers, artists, bloggers, and content creators who want better audience insights, monetization features, and flexible messaging tools.

Steps to Switch to a Business or Creator Account

Switching to a Business or Creator account is a simple process that takes just a few minutes. Follow these steps:

1. **Open Instagram and Go to Settings**
   - Tap your profile picture at the bottom right to go to your profile.
   - Tap the three horizontal lines (menu) in the top right corner.
   - Select Settings and privacy.

2. **Navigate to Account Type Options**
   - Scroll down and tap Account type and tools.
   - Select Switch to professional account.

3. **Choose Your Account Type**
   - Instagram will present two options: **Business** or **Creator**.
   - Choose the one that best aligns with your goals.

4. **Select a Category**

   o You will be prompted to choose a category that represents your business or brand (e.g., Entrepreneur, Blogger, Fashion Brand, Public Figure, etc.).

   o This category will appear on your profile unless you choose to hide it.

5. **Set Up Contact Information**

   o Instagram allows you to add business contact details such as email, phone number, and physical address.

   o This makes it easier for customers or followers to reach out.

6. **Connect to a Facebook Page (Optional but Recommended)**

   o If you want to run Instagram ads, integrate Instagram Shopping, or use cross-platform promotions, linking a Facebook Page is advisable.

   o You can either connect to an existing page or create a new one.

7. **Complete the Setup Process**

   o Instagram may prompt you to explore professional tools like **Insights, Promotions, and Shopping**.

   o Tap **Done** to finalize the switch.

Key Benefits of Using a Business or Creator Account

Switching to a Business or Creator account unlocks several advantages:

1. Access to Instagram Insights

- Get in-depth analytics on follower demographics, engagement, and content performance.

- Track which posts perform best and adjust your strategy accordingly.

2. Professional Contact Options

- Add buttons like **Call, Email, or Directions** to make it easier for customers to reach you.

- Enhance credibility by presenting a professional online presence.

3. Ability to Run Instagram Ads

- Promote posts to reach a wider audience and increase engagement.
- Set up **targeted ad campaigns** using Instagram's advanced advertising tools.

4. Instagram Shopping (For Business Accounts)

- Tag products in your posts and stories.
- Enable users to purchase directly through Instagram.

5. Saved Replies (For Business Accounts)

- Respond to common customer inquiries quickly with pre-saved responses.

6. Flexible Messaging Tools (For Creator Accounts)

- Organize DMs into **Primary, General, and Requests** for better communication.
- Prioritize messages from important followers or brand collaborations.

7. Monetization Opportunities (For Creator Accounts)

- Gain access to **Brand Collabs Manager**, allowing brands to find and partner with you.
- Use features like **Instagram Badges** during live streams to earn money.

Common Challenges and How to Overcome Them

1. Limited Music Library for Business Accounts

- Instagram restricts music usage for Business accounts due to copyright licensing.
- **Solution**: Use royalty-free music or switch to a Creator account if music access is a priority.

2. Need for Constant Engagement

- Professional accounts require active engagement to maximize reach.
- **Solution**: Schedule content in advance and interact with followers daily.

3. Ads Require Budget and Optimization

- Running Instagram ads can be costly if not optimized correctly.

- **Solution**: Start with small budgets, analyze performance, and scale accordingly.

5. Final Thoughts

Switching to a Business or Creator account is a crucial step toward leveraging Instagram for brand growth, monetization, and audience engagement. Whether you're a company looking to boost sales or a content creator aiming for more visibility, Instagram's professional tools provide the necessary resources to succeed. Take advantage of insights, advertising, and shopping features to maximize your Instagram presence and build a sustainable online brand.

5.1.2 Setting Up Instagram Shopping

Introduction to Instagram Shopping

Instagram Shopping is a powerful feature that allows businesses to showcase and sell their products directly through Instagram. With millions of users engaging with content daily, Instagram has become a leading platform for social commerce. Setting up Instagram Shopping enables businesses to create a seamless shopping experience, making it easy for users to discover, explore, and purchase products without leaving the app.

This section will guide you through the process of setting up Instagram Shopping, from meeting eligibility requirements to launching your first shoppable post.

1. Understanding Instagram Shopping

Instagram Shopping is designed to help businesses turn their profiles into online storefronts. With features like product tags, shoppable posts, and Instagram Checkout (in some regions), businesses can drive direct sales from their Instagram feed.

Key Features of Instagram Shopping:

- **Product Tags:** Allows businesses to tag products in posts and stories.

- **Instagram Shop:** A dedicated shopping tab where users can browse and purchase products.

- **Instagram Checkout:** Enables users to buy products directly within Instagram (available in select countries).

- **Collections:** Lets businesses group similar products for easy browsing.

- **Product Detail Pages:** Provide essential information about items, including pricing and descriptions.

2. Eligibility Requirements for Instagram Shopping

Before setting up Instagram Shopping, ensure your business meets Instagram's eligibility criteria.

Basic Requirements:

- You must be located in a supported market.

- Your business must sell physical goods that comply with Instagram's commerce policies.

- You need a **business or creator account** on Instagram.

- Your Instagram account must be linked to a **Facebook Page**.

- You must have a **Facebook Commerce Manager** account.

- Your website must be owned and operated by you, and all products must be available for direct purchase.

3. Step-by-Step Guide to Setting Up Instagram Shopping

Step 1: Convert to a Business or Creator Account

If you haven't already, switch to a **business or creator account**:

1. Go to **Settings** on your Instagram profile.

2. Select **Account > Switch to Professional Account**.

3. Choose **Business** or **Creator**.

4. Connect to a **Facebook Page** (or create one if you don't have it).

5. Complete your business details and category selection.

Step 2: Connect to a Facebook Commerce Manager

Instagram Shopping relies on **Facebook Commerce Manager** to manage your catalog. Here's how to set it up:

1. Go to <u>Facebook Commerce Manager</u>.

2. Click **Create a Commerce Account** and choose your **Business Manager account**.

3. Select **Set Up a Shop** and follow the on-screen instructions.

4. Connect your Instagram account under the **Sales Channels** section.

Step 3: Add a Product Catalog

Your products need to be stored in a Facebook Catalog before you can tag them on Instagram.

Option 1: Using Facebook Business Manager

1. Open **Facebook Business Manager** and go to **Commerce Manager**.

2. Click **Catalogs > Create Catalog**.

3. Choose **E-commerce** and click **Next**.

4. Select **Upload Product Info** manually or sync from an e-commerce platform (like Shopify or WooCommerce).

5. Add product details including name, description, price, and images.

Option 2: Using an E-Commerce Integration

If you're using Shopify, WooCommerce, or another supported platform, you can integrate directly with Facebook Shop. This automatically syncs your product catalog with Instagram Shopping.

Step 4: Submit Your Account for Review

Instagram requires businesses to undergo an approval process before enabling Shopping features.

1. Go to **Settings > Business > Set Up Instagram Shopping**.

2. Follow the instructions and submit your account for review.

3. Instagram typically reviews applications within **a few days**, but it may take longer.

4. You'll receive a notification in **Business Settings** once approved.

Step 5: Turn on Instagram Shopping

Once approved, enable Instagram Shopping:

1. Go to **Settings > Business**.

2. Tap **Shopping**.

3. Select your **Product Catalog**.

4. Tap **Done**.

---

4. Creating Shoppable Content on Instagram

Now that Instagram Shopping is set up, you can start tagging products in your posts and stories.

Adding Product Tags in Feed Posts

1. Upload a new post as usual.

2. Tap **Tag Products**.

3. Select the product from your catalog.

4. Publish the post.

Adding Product Stickers in Stories

1. Open Instagram Stories and upload content.

2. Tap the **Sticker icon** and choose **Product Sticker**.

3. Select a product from your catalog.

4. Customize the sticker and place it on your story.

5. Share your story.

Using Instagram Live Shopping *(if available in your region)*

1. Start an Instagram Live session.

2. Tap the **Shopping Bag icon**.

3. Select a product from your catalog to feature.

4. Viewers can tap the product to purchase while watching.

5. Best Practices for Instagram Shopping Success

- **Use High-Quality Images:** Showcase products with clear, professional visuals.

- **Optimize Product Descriptions:** Include detailed, engaging text and pricing.

- **Leverage User-Generated Content:** Encourage customers to share photos and reviews.

- **Promote Your Instagram Shop:** Use reels, stories, and collaborations to drive traffic.

- **Monitor Insights:** Use Instagram Shopping analytics to track sales and improve performance.

Conclusion

Setting up Instagram Shopping unlocks a world of opportunities for businesses looking to expand their e-commerce presence. By following these steps, you can turn your Instagram account into a powerful sales channel, driving engagement and revenue directly from the platform.

Once your shop is live, experiment with different strategies, track your performance, and refine your approach to maximize success!

5.1.3 Using Instagram for Personal Branding

Introduction

In today's digital age, personal branding has become an essential component of career success, entrepreneurship, and thought leadership. Instagram, with its highly visual nature and massive global user base, is one of the most powerful platforms for building and growing a personal brand. Whether you're an influencer, entrepreneur, artist, or industry expert, Instagram allows you to showcase your expertise, connect with your audience, and establish credibility in your niche.

This section will guide you through the key steps and strategies to effectively use Instagram for personal branding.

Understanding Personal Branding on Instagram

Personal branding is about crafting and communicating your unique identity, values, and expertise to a target audience. It is the process of shaping public perception to reflect your skills, personality, and professional or personal mission.

On Instagram, personal branding is driven by:

- **Visual storytelling**: High-quality images, videos, and graphics to share your message.
- **Authenticity**: Being real and relatable to create trust and engagement.
- **Consistency**: Posting regularly and maintaining a cohesive style and message.
- **Engagement**: Actively interacting with your followers to build a community.
- **Value-driven content**: Providing information, entertainment, or inspiration to your audience.

Setting Up Your Instagram for Personal Branding

1. Choosing the Right Instagram Handle and Profile Name

Your Instagram handle and profile name should reflect your personal brand. Ideally, use your real name or a recognizable variation of it.

- Example: If your name is Jane Doe, your handle could be **@janedoeofficial** or **@janedoecoach**.
- Avoid random numbers or characters that make your handle look unprofessional.

2. Crafting an Engaging Bio

Your Instagram bio is one of the first things people see when they visit your profile. It should clearly state who you are, what you do, and why people should follow you.

- Use a strong headline (e.g., **"Helping Entrepreneurs Build Profitable Brands"**).

- Include keywords related to your niche.

- Add a call-to-action (e.g., **"DM me for business inquiries"**).

- Utilize the link section to direct followers to your website, blog, or a landing page.

3. Choosing the Right Profile Picture

Your profile picture should be professional and easily recognizable. It should be:

- A high-resolution headshot.

- Bright and clear, avoiding overly busy backgrounds.

- Consistent across other social media platforms for brand recognition.

Creating a Content Strategy for Personal Branding

A strong content strategy is key to building your personal brand on Instagram.

1. Define Your Content Pillars

Content pillars are the core topics you consistently post about. Choose 3-5 main themes that align with your personal brand. For example:

- **Entrepreneurship**: Business tips, startup advice, financial growth.

- **Personal Development**: Mindset, habits, productivity.

- **Behind the Scenes**: Daily life, work processes, personal hobbies.

- **Success Stories**: Client testimonials, personal achievements.

- **Motivation & Inspiration**: Quotes, lessons learned, challenges overcome.

2. Plan Your Content Types

To keep your audience engaged, mix up different content formats:

- **Feed posts**: High-quality images, carousels, and videos.

- **Instagram Stories**: Behind-the-scenes, daily updates, Q&A sessions.
- **Reels**: Short, engaging videos with educational or entertaining value.
- **IGTV & Live Streams**: In-depth discussions, interviews, or live coaching sessions.

3. Use a Consistent Visual Style

- Choose a cohesive color scheme and aesthetic.
- Use consistent filters or presets.
- Ensure text, graphics, and branding elements align with your brand identity.

Growing Your Personal Brand on Instagram

1. Building an Engaged Community

- Respond to comments and DMs to show your audience you value them.
- Ask questions in captions to encourage interaction.
- Use Instagram Stories to engage through polls, quizzes, and stickers.
- Join relevant conversations by commenting on other industry leaders' posts.

2. Leveraging Hashtags and Geotags

- Use a mix of niche-specific, industry, and trending hashtags.
- Research hashtags that your target audience follows.
- Geotag your posts to attract local followers.

3. Collaborating with Others

- Partner with influencers or brands that align with your values.
- Do Instagram Lives with experts in your field.
- Participate in shoutout exchanges with like-minded creators.

Monetizing Your Personal Brand on Instagram

1. Sponsored Content

- Partner with brands that align with your personal brand.

- Clearly disclose partnerships with #ad or #sponsored.

- Ensure your content remains authentic and valuable to your audience.

2. Selling Your Own Products or Services

- Promote digital products, courses, or coaching services.

- Use Instagram Shopping to sell physical products.

- Offer exclusive content through subscriptions.

3. Affiliate Marketing

- Share affiliate links to products you genuinely recommend.

- Use Instagram Stories with Swipe Up links (for accounts with over 10K followers) or link in bio.

- Provide honest reviews and tutorials to increase conversions.

Measuring Success and Optimizing Your Strategy

1. Tracking Key Metrics

Use Instagram Insights to monitor:

- **Follower Growth**: How fast your audience is growing.

- **Engagement Rate**: Likes, comments, shares, and saves.

- **Reach and Impressions**: How many people see your content.

- **Click-Through Rate (CTR)**: How often people click your bio link.

2. Adapting Your Strategy

- Analyze what types of posts perform best and adjust accordingly.

- Experiment with different posting times and formats.

- Stay updated with Instagram algorithm changes and trends.

Conclusion

Instagram is a powerful tool for personal branding when used strategically. By optimizing your profile, creating valuable content, engaging with your audience, and leveraging monetization opportunities, you can establish yourself as an authority in your field and build a successful personal brand.

Now, it's time to take action! Define your niche, refine your content strategy, and start growing your influence on Instagram today.

5.2 Instagram Ads and Promotions

5.2.1 How Instagram Ads Work

Instagram has evolved into one of the most powerful digital marketing platforms, with over a billion active users and a highly engaged audience. Businesses, influencers, and entrepreneurs leverage Instagram ads to reach their target audience, build brand awareness, and drive sales. In this section, we will explore how Instagram ads work, the different types of ads available, and best practices to create high-performing advertisements.

Understanding Instagram Ads

Instagram ads are paid promotions that appear within the platform's feed, stories, Explore section, and Reels. These ads allow businesses to target specific audiences based on demographics, interests, behaviors, and more. Instagram ads are managed through Facebook's Ads Manager, providing detailed analytics and optimization options to improve ad performance.

How Do Instagram Ads Appear?

Instagram ads blend seamlessly into the user experience, appearing in various locations such as:

- **Feed Ads**: Sponsored posts that look like regular content but include a "Sponsored" label.
- **Story Ads**: Full-screen ads that appear between users' stories.
- **Explore Ads**: Ads that appear in the Explore section, targeting users looking for new content.
- **Reels Ads**: Short video ads displayed in the Reels feed.
- **Shopping Ads**: Clickable product ads that direct users to an online store.

Each format serves a different purpose, and businesses choose the most suitable option based on their advertising goals.

The Instagram Ads Auction System

Instagram ads operate on an auction-based system, where advertisers bid for placements based on their campaign objectives. The cost of an ad depends on several factors, including:

- **Audience targeting**: Highly competitive audiences have higher costs.

- **Ad placement**: Ads shown in premium spots (e.g., Instagram Stories) may have higher costs.

- **Ad quality and relevance**: Instagram rewards high-quality, engaging ads with lower costs per click (CPC) or impression (CPM).

- **Bidding strategy**: Advertisers can choose between automatic and manual bidding.

The auction system ensures that the most relevant and engaging ads reach the right audience while optimizing advertiser budgets.

Types of Instagram Ads

1. Photo Ads

Photo ads use a single image to capture attention. These ads work best for businesses showcasing products, services, or brand messages in a visually appealing way.

2. Video Ads

Video ads can be up to 60 seconds long and are designed to tell a story, demonstrate a product, or create brand awareness. High-quality videos with engaging content tend to perform well.

3. Carousel Ads

Carousel ads allow users to swipe through multiple images or videos within a single ad. These are ideal for showcasing a collection of products, step-by-step guides, or different features of a service.

4. Story Ads

Instagram Story ads are full-screen vertical ads that appear between organic stories. They often include interactive elements like polls, swipe-up links, and GIFs to enhance engagement.

5. Explore Ads

These ads appear within the Explore section, where users discover new content. Explore ads are effective for reaching new audiences interested in specific niches.

6. Reels Ads

Reels ads are short-form video ads that play within the Reels feed. These are great for brands looking to tap into Instagram's growing short-video trend.

7. Shopping Ads

Shopping ads showcase products directly in the Instagram feed, allowing users to click and purchase seamlessly. These ads integrate with Instagram Shops, making the buying process smoother.

Setting Up Instagram Ads

To create an Instagram ad, follow these steps:

1. **Access Facebook Ads Manager**: Instagram ads are managed through Facebook's ad platform.

2. **Choose Your Campaign Objective**: Options include brand awareness, website traffic, lead generation, and conversions.

3. **Define Your Target Audience**: Set parameters such as location, age, gender, interests, and behaviors.

4. **Select Ad Placement**: Choose whether to run ads on Instagram Feed, Stories, Reels, or Explore.

5. **Set Your Budget and Schedule**: Decide on daily or lifetime budgets and choose the duration of the campaign.

6. **Design Your Ad**: Upload images or videos, write engaging ad copy, and include a clear call to action (CTA).

7. **Launch and Monitor Performance**: Use Instagram Insights and Facebook Ads Manager to track metrics and optimize the ad campaign.

Best Practices for Instagram Ads

- **Use High-Quality Visuals**: Instagram is a visual platform, so ensure your ads stand out.

- **Write Engaging Captions**: Keep them concise and persuasive.

- **Leverage Instagram's Ad Targeting**: Define your audience for better ad performance.

- **Include a Clear Call-to-Action (CTA)**: Guide users on the next steps, such as "Shop Now" or "Learn More."

- **Test Different Ad Formats**: A/B testing helps find the most effective ad creatives.

- **Analyze Performance Metrics**: Adjust strategies based on engagement, reach, and conversion rates.

Conclusion

Instagram ads provide an incredible opportunity for brands and businesses to reach their target audience effectively. By understanding how Instagram ads work, selecting the right ad format, and following best practices, advertisers can maximize their return on investment (ROI) and achieve their marketing goals. In the next section, we will explore how to create a successful Instagram ad campaign step by step.

5.2.2 Creating Your First Instagram Ad

Instagram Ads provide a powerful way to reach a targeted audience, increase engagement, and drive business results. Whether you're looking to gain followers, boost brand awareness, or sell products, Instagram Ads can help you achieve your goals. In this section, we will walk you through the step-by-step process of creating your first Instagram ad.

Step 1: Define Your Advertising Objective

Before setting up your ad, it is crucial to determine what you want to achieve. Instagram offers several ad objectives, including:

- **Brand Awareness:** Increase recognition of your brand among potential customers.

- **Reach:** Maximize the number of people who see your ad.

- **Traffic:** Drive users to your website, app, or Instagram profile.

- **Engagement:** Get more likes, comments, shares, and video views.

- **Lead Generation:** Collect contact information from interested users.

- **Conversions:** Encourage people to take specific actions, such as purchasing a product or signing up for a service.

Selecting the right objective ensures your ad performs effectively and aligns with your marketing goals.

Step 2: Choose Your Ad Format

Instagram provides multiple ad formats tailored to different campaign needs:

- **Photo Ads:** A single image with a caption and call-to-action (CTA).

- **Video Ads:** Short videos (up to 60 seconds) that capture attention.

- **Carousel Ads:** Multiple images or videos in one ad that users can swipe through.

- **Stories Ads:** Full-screen vertical ads appearing in Instagram Stories.

- **Reels Ads:** Short-form video ads displayed in the Instagram Reels section.

- **Collection Ads:** A combination of images and videos to create an immersive shopping experience.

Choose the format that best suits your content and advertising goal.

Step 3: Set Up Your Instagram Ad Using Meta Ads Manager

Meta Ads Manager (formerly Facebook Ads Manager) is the primary tool for creating and managing Instagram Ads. Follow these steps to set up your ad:

1. Access Meta Ads Manager

- Log in to your Facebook Business account.

- Navigate to **Ads Manager** by clicking on the menu in the top left corner.

- Click **Create** to start a new ad campaign.

2. Select Your Campaign Objective

- Choose an objective that aligns with your marketing goal.

- Click **Continue** to proceed.

3. Define Your Target Audience

Targeting the right audience ensures your ad reaches people most likely to engage. Use the following parameters:

- **Location:** Target users based on country, city, or a specific radius.

- **Demographics:** Select age, gender, and language preferences.

- **Interests:** Target users based on their Instagram activity, such as interests in fashion, fitness, travel, etc.

- **Behavior:** Reach people based on purchase behavior and device usage.

- **Custom Audiences:** Retarget people who have interacted with your brand before.

- **Lookalike Audiences:** Find new users similar to your existing customers.

4. Choose Ad Placements

- **Automatic Placements (Recommended):** Meta's AI places your ad where it is most effective across Facebook and Instagram.

- **Manual Placements:** Select specific placements such as Instagram Stories, Instagram Feed, or Instagram Reels.

5. Set Your Budget and Schedule

- **Daily Budget:** The maximum amount you want to spend per day.

- **Lifetime Budget:** A total budget for the entire campaign.

- **Ad Schedule:** Choose to run ads continuously or during specific time periods.

Step 4: Create Your Ad Content

Once your campaign is set up, it's time to create compelling content that captures attention and drives engagement.

1. Choose Your Creative (Image or Video)

- Use **high-quality visuals** to grab attention.
- Keep videos between **6-15 seconds** for better performance.
- Use Instagram's built-in tools to edit and enhance images.

2. Write a Captivating Caption

- Keep it **concise and engaging**.
- Include a **strong call-to-action (CTA)** like "Shop Now," "Learn More," or "Sign Up."
- Use **relevant hashtags** to expand reach.

3. Add a Call-to-Action Button

Instagram offers various CTA buttons depending on your ad objective:

- "Shop Now"
- "Sign Up"
- "Learn More"
- "Get Offer"
- "Contact Us"

Step 5: Review and Publish Your Ad

Before publishing, double-check your ad settings:

- Ensure **the correct objective and audience** are selected.
- Review **ad placements** to confirm they align with your strategy.
- Check for **spelling errors** in captions and CTAs.
- Click **Publish** to launch your ad.

Step 6: Monitor and Optimize Your Ad Performance

Once your ad is live, monitoring its performance is essential. Use **Meta Ads Manager** to track:

- **Impressions:** How many times your ad was displayed.

- **Engagement:** Likes, comments, shares, and saves.

- **Click-Through Rate (CTR):** The percentage of users who clicked on your ad.

- **Conversion Rate:** How many users completed the desired action.

- **Cost Per Result (CPR):** The amount spent per click, view, or conversion.

Tips for Optimization:

- **A/B Test Different Ad Variations:** Try different images, captions, and CTA buttons to see what works best.

- **Adjust Targeting Settings:** Refine your audience based on performance insights.

- **Change Posting Times:** Experiment with different times to maximize reach.

- **Increase Budget for High-Performing Ads:** If an ad performs well, allocate more budget to it.

Conclusion

Creating your first Instagram ad may seem complex, but by following these steps, you can efficiently set up, launch, and optimize a successful campaign. With the right objectives, engaging content, and strategic targeting, your Instagram ads can help you grow your brand and achieve your marketing goals.

5.2.3 Measuring Ad Performance

Introduction

Running Instagram ads is just the first step toward a successful marketing strategy. To ensure your campaigns are effective, you must continuously measure and analyze their performance. Instagram provides a robust set of analytics tools to track ad performance, understand audience engagement, and optimize for better results. This section will guide you through the key metrics, tools, and best practices for measuring your Instagram ad performance.

1. Understanding Instagram Ad Metrics

Instagram's ad performance is measured using several key metrics that help advertisers assess engagement, reach, and return on investment (ROI). Below are the most critical metrics you should track:

Reach and Impressions

- **Reach:** The number of unique users who have seen your ad.

- **Impressions:** The total number of times your ad has been displayed, including multiple views by the same user.

- **Why it matters:** A high reach ensures your ad is exposed to a broad audience, while impressions indicate how frequently users see your ad.

Click-Through Rate (CTR)

- **CTR:** The percentage of users who clicked on your ad after seeing it.

- **Formula:** (Total Clicks / Total Impressions) × 100

- **Why it matters:** A high CTR suggests your ad is engaging and compelling enough to prompt user action.

Engagement Rate

- **Includes:** Likes, comments, shares, and saves on your ad.

- **Why it matters:** High engagement indicates that your content resonates with your audience, which can improve ad performance through Instagram's algorithm.

Conversion Rate

- **Conversion:** The percentage of users who completed a desired action (e.g., making a purchase, signing up, or downloading an app) after clicking on your ad.

- **Why it matters:** A strong conversion rate shows that your ad successfully encourages users to take action.

Cost Per Click (CPC) and Cost Per Impression (CPM)

- **CPC:** The amount you pay for each click on your ad.

- **CPM:** The amount you pay per 1,000 impressions.

- **Why it matters:** Keeping CPC and CPM low ensures cost-effective ad spending while maximizing visibility.

Return on Ad Spend (ROAS)

- **ROAS:** The revenue generated from your ad campaign divided by the amount spent on the ads.

- **Formula:** Revenue from Ads / Ad Spend

- **Why it matters:** A high ROAS means your campaign is generating a profitable return.

2. Using Instagram Insights for Ad Analysis

Instagram provides built-in analytics tools to help advertisers track performance.

Accessing Instagram Insights

- Navigate to your Instagram **Business or Creator Account**.

- Go to **Professional Dashboard** and select **Insights**.

- Click on **Ad Insights** to view performance data.

Key Sections in Instagram Insights

- **Overview Tab:** Provides general ad performance metrics, including reach, impressions, and engagement.

- **Content Tab:** Shows performance for individual ads, including interactions and audience demographics.

- **Activity Tab:** Displays actions users take, such as website visits, profile clicks, or link clicks from ads.

3. Third-Party Analytics Tools

While Instagram Insights is useful, third-party tools provide deeper insights and integration with other platforms.

Facebook Ads Manager

- **Why use it?** More comprehensive data, A/B testing features, and audience segmentation.

- **Key Metrics Available:** ROI, detailed demographics, cost breakdown, and campaign comparison.

Google Analytics

- **Why use it?** Tracks Instagram ad traffic on your website and measures conversions.

- **Key Features:** UTM tracking, bounce rates, session duration, and conversion funnels.

Other Tools

- **Hootsuite Ads** (for scheduling and managing Instagram ad campaigns).

- **Sprout Social** (for in-depth engagement and competitor analysis).

- **SEMrush** (for ad tracking and SEO insights).

---

4. Best Practices for Measuring and Optimizing Performance

Set Clear Objectives

Before analyzing ad performance, define your goals. Are you aiming for brand awareness, lead generation, or sales? Your KPIs should align with these objectives.

A/B Testing Your Ads

- **What is A/B Testing?** Running two versions of an ad with slight variations (e.g., different images, copy, or CTA) to see which performs better.

- **Why use it?** Identifies which elements resonate most with your audience.

Optimize Based on Data

- If **CTR is low**, refine your ad visuals and headlines.

- If **engagement is poor**, experiment with different formats (e.g., video vs. carousel posts).

- If **conversion rate is low**, adjust landing pages or call-to-action (CTA) buttons.

Monitor Ad Frequency

- **What is it?** The average number of times a user sees your ad.
- **Ideal range:** Between 1.5 to 3. Too high may lead to ad fatigue, while too low may reduce impact.

Adjust Budget Allocation

- **If an ad is performing well**, increase the budget to maximize results.
- **If an ad underperforms**, reallocate funds to better-performing ads.

Conclusion

Measuring Instagram ad performance is crucial for ensuring a strong return on investment and optimizing future campaigns. By tracking key metrics such as CTR, engagement rate, conversion rate, and ROAS, you can make data-driven decisions that enhance your ad effectiveness. Use Instagram Insights, Facebook Ads Manager, and other third-party tools to analyze performance and continuously refine your strategy. Implementing A/B testing, monitoring ad frequency, and adjusting budgets will further improve your Instagram ad success.

By applying these best practices, you can maximize the impact of your Instagram ads and achieve your marketing goals with greater efficiency.

5.3 Collaborations and Partnerships

5.3.1 Working with Influencers

Introduction to Influencer Marketing

Influencer marketing has become one of the most effective ways to reach and engage audiences on Instagram. By collaborating with influencers, brands can tap into established communities, increase brand awareness, and drive conversions. But working with influencers requires a strategic approach to ensure authenticity, effectiveness, and return on investment.

Understanding Influencer Tiers

Not all influencers are the same, and choosing the right one for your brand depends on your goals and budget. Influencers are generally categorized into different tiers based on their follower count:

- **Nano-Influencers (1K-10K followers)** – Highly engaged communities, great for niche marketing, and ideal for startups and small businesses.

- **Micro-Influencers (10K-100K followers)** – Well-connected with their audience, often seen as more authentic, and good for increasing engagement.

- **Macro-Influencers (100K-1M followers)** – A broader reach, higher visibility, and more expensive to work with.

- **Mega-Influencers (1M+ followers)** – Celebrity-level exposure, but engagement rates may be lower compared to smaller influencers.

Choosing the right influencer tier depends on your objectives. If your goal is brand awareness, macro- or mega-influencers may be suitable. If engagement and trust-building are your focus, micro- or nano-influencers are often more effective.

Finding the Right Influencers

Before reaching out to influencers, ensure they align with your brand values and audience. Here's how to find the right influencers:

1. **Use Instagram's Search & Hashtags** – Search for industry-specific hashtags to find influencers posting relevant content.

2. **Check Engagement Rates** – Look at likes, comments, and shares rather than just follower count.

3. **Analyze Audience Demographics** – Use tools like Instagram Insights or influencer marketing platforms to check audience location, age, and interests.

4. **Review Past Brand Collaborations** – Ensure the influencer's previous partnerships align with your brand image.

5. **Use Influencer Marketing Platforms** – Platforms like Upfluence, AspireIQ, and Heepsy can help identify suitable influencers.

Approaching and Negotiating with Influencers

Once you've identified the right influencers, the next step is outreach and negotiation.

1. **Personalized Outreach** – Avoid generic messages; personalize your pitch to show you've done your research.

2. **Clearly Define Expectations** – Outline deliverables, such as post formats, timelines, and campaign goals.

3. **Discuss Compensation** – Influencers may accept different forms of payment:

   o Monetary payment (fixed fees or performance-based commissions)

   o Free products or services

   o Affiliate marketing partnerships

4. **Negotiate Terms** – Consider exclusivity clauses, content ownership, and the duration of the partnership.

5. **Sign a Contract** – Protect both parties by clearly defining terms in a formal agreement.

Types of Influencer Collaborations

There are several ways to collaborate with influencers on Instagram:

1. **Sponsored Posts** – The influencer creates a post featuring your product or service.

2. **Instagram Stories & Reels** – Short-form content that can include product demonstrations or testimonials.

3. **Giveaways & Contests** – Engaging campaigns where influencers encourage followers to participate for a chance to win a prize.

4. **Affiliate Marketing** – The influencer earns a commission for sales made through their unique referral link or discount code.

5. **Brand Ambassadorships** – Long-term partnerships where influencers consistently promote your brand over time.

Measuring Influencer Campaign Success

Tracking the performance of influencer collaborations is crucial to understanding ROI. Key performance indicators (KPIs) to measure include:

- **Engagement Rate** – Likes, comments, shares, and saves on influencer posts.

- **Reach and Impressions** – How many users saw the content.

- **Follower Growth** – Increase in your Instagram followers due to influencer collaboration.

- **Website Traffic** – Click-through rates from influencer content to your website or landing pages.

- **Conversion Rates** – The number of purchases or sign-ups generated through influencer promotions.

Using tracking tools like UTM parameters, Instagram Insights, and third-party analytics platforms can help you measure the effectiveness of your influencer campaigns.

Common Mistakes to Avoid

When working with influencers, avoid these common pitfalls:

- **Choosing Influencers Solely Based on Follower Count** – Engagement and audience relevance matter more.

- **Not Setting Clear Expectations** – Misaligned goals can lead to unsuccessful campaigns.

- **Ignoring FTC Guidelines** – Ensure influencers disclose sponsored content using #ad or #sponsored to comply with regulations.

- **Overlooking Authenticity** – If an influencer's promotion feels forced, it can harm brand credibility.

Conclusion

Influencer marketing is a powerful tool for growing your brand on Instagram when done strategically. By selecting the right influencers, establishing clear goals, and continuously analyzing performance, businesses can build strong, authentic relationships with their audience. Whether working with nano-influencers for targeted engagement or macro-influencers for mass exposure, influencer collaborations can be a game-changer in your Instagram marketing strategy.

5.3.2 Running Giveaways and Contests

Introduction

Giveaways and contests are powerful tools for boosting engagement, attracting new followers, and increasing brand awareness on Instagram. When done correctly, they can create excitement around your brand, encourage user participation, and generate organic reach. In this section, we will explore the key elements of successful Instagram giveaways and contests, from planning and execution to measuring results.

Why Run a Giveaway or Contest on Instagram?

Running an Instagram giveaway or contest offers several benefits:

- **Increased Engagement**: Users are more likely to like, comment, and share posts that involve a prize.

- **Follower Growth**: Well-structured contests can attract new followers who are interested in your content.

- **Brand Awareness**: Giveaways create buzz and encourage participants to share your brand with their network.

- **User-Generated Content (UGC)**: Some contests encourage users to create content featuring your products, which can be repurposed for marketing.

- **Lead Generation**: You can use giveaways to collect email addresses and other customer information.

Types of Instagram Giveaways and Contests

There are different types of contests you can run based on your objectives:

1. Like, Comment, and Follow Contests

- Users must like the post, follow your account, and comment on the post to enter.
- Great for boosting engagement and increasing your follower count.

2. Tag a Friend Contests

- Participants tag one or more friends in the comments to enter.
- Helps expand reach and attract new potential followers.

3. Photo or Video Submission Contests

- Users create and post their own content using a branded hashtag.
- Encourages user-generated content and enhances brand authenticity.

4. Story-Based Contests

- Users participate by sharing your contest post in their Instagram Stories.
- Ideal for increasing visibility and reaching a wider audience.

5. Hashtag Contests

- Participants use a specific hashtag in their posts to enter.
- Helps track contest entries and increases brand exposure.

Planning a Successful Instagram Giveaway

To maximize the effectiveness of your contest, follow these key steps:

1. Define Your Goal

Before launching a contest, determine what you want to achieve:

- More followers?
- Increased engagement?

- Brand awareness?

- User-generated content?

2. Choose a Relevant Prize

The prize should align with your brand and be attractive to your target audience. Some ideas include:

- Your own products or services

- Exclusive discounts or bundles

- Gift cards

- Collaborations with influencers for larger giveaways

3. Set Clear Rules and Guidelines

Ensure that the contest rules are easy to understand and follow. Include:

- Entry requirements (e.g., follow, like, comment, tag)

- Contest duration

- Eligibility criteria (e.g., location restrictions)

- Winner selection method

- How the winner will be contacted

4. Create an Eye-Catching Contest Post

Your contest announcement post should include:

- A high-quality image or video

- Clear and concise instructions

- A compelling call-to-action ("Enter now!")

- Relevant hashtags (e.g., #Giveaway, #Contest, #WinWithUs)

5. Promote Your Contest

Use multiple channels to promote your giveaway:

- **Instagram Stories**: Post updates and reminders

- **Collaborations**: Partner with influencers or brands to reach a wider audience
- **Paid Ads**: Boost your post to target specific demographics
- **Cross-Promotion**: Share on other social media platforms or email newsletters

6. Monitor Engagement and Entries

Track participation through:

- Instagram Insights (likes, comments, shares, saves)
- Third-party tools (e.g., Gleam, Rafflecopter)
- Manual tracking if necessary

7. Selecting and Announcing Winners

- Use a random selection tool if it's a luck-based giveaway.
- If it's a contest requiring creativity, have a judging panel.
- Announce the winner publicly and contact them directly.
- Encourage the winner to share their prize to boost credibility.

8. Analyze Results and Optimize Future Giveaways

After the contest ends, evaluate performance:

- Did you achieve your goal?
- Which aspects worked well?
- What could be improved for the next giveaway?

Common Mistakes to Avoid

1. **Unclear Rules**: Complicated instructions lead to low participation.
2. **Irrelevant Prizes**: Generic prizes attract random participants who may not be interested in your brand.
3. **Ignoring Instagram's Rules**: Violating Instagram's policies can lead to account restrictions.

4. **Not Promoting Enough**: Relying only on one post limits reach.

5. **Not Following Through**: Failing to deliver the prize damages credibility.

Conclusion

Instagram giveaways and contests are excellent tools for engagement and growth when executed correctly. By carefully planning, promoting, and analyzing your contest, you can create a fun and rewarding experience for your audience while strengthening your brand's presence on Instagram. Ready to launch your first giveaway? Start planning today and watch your engagement soar!

5.3.3 Sponsorships and Brand Deals

Introduction

Instagram has become a powerful platform for influencer marketing, making brand sponsorships and deals a lucrative opportunity for content creators. Whether you are a micro-influencer or have a massive following, working with brands can provide financial rewards, increase your credibility, and help you grow your audience. However, successful sponsorships require strategic planning, professional communication, and a deep understanding of your audience and brand alignment.

In this section, we will explore how to secure sponsorships, negotiate deals, maintain authenticity, and comply with legal requirements when engaging in brand partnerships on Instagram.

1. Understanding Sponsorships and Brand Deals

Brand deals and sponsorships come in various forms, including:

- **Sponsored Posts** – A brand pays you to create content featuring their product or service.

- **Affiliate Marketing** – You promote a brand's product and earn a commission for every sale made through your referral link.

- **Product Seeding** – Brands send free products in exchange for exposure, with or without financial compensation.

- **Long-Term Partnerships** – A brand hires you as an ambassador for an extended period, offering consistent collaboration and exclusivity.

- **Paid Stories, Reels, and Live Streams** – Brands may pay for promotion through Instagram Stories, short-form videos (Reels), or live streams.

- **Event Collaborations** – You attend or host brand-related events, sometimes with travel expenses covered.

Understanding these different formats will help you choose partnerships that align with your content style and audience.

2. Building a Strong Personal Brand

Before brands approach you—or before you pitch yourself to them—you must establish a strong personal brand. Here's how:

Define Your Niche

Brands want to collaborate with influencers whose audiences match their target market. Whether you focus on fashion, fitness, travel, beauty, tech, or another industry, your content should clearly define your expertise.

Maintain High-Quality Content

Visual appeal is everything on Instagram. High-resolution images, well-edited videos, and professional storytelling can make your profile stand out to brands.

Engage With Your Audience

A strong engagement rate (likes, comments, shares, and saves) is more valuable than a high follower count. Brands prioritize influencers who foster genuine interactions with their audience.

Consistency and Authenticity

Posting consistently and being authentic in your recommendations make you more attractive to potential brand partners. Brands look for influencers who seamlessly integrate products into their lifestyle.

3. Finding and Securing Sponsorships

Once your profile is optimized, you can start seeking brand collaborations.

Reaching Out to Brands

While some brands may approach you, proactive outreach is often necessary. Here's how to contact brands effectively:

- **Identify Suitable Brands** – Choose companies that align with your niche and audience.

- **Craft a Strong Pitch** – Introduce yourself, highlight your engagement rates, and explain why you're a great fit.

- **Provide Media Kits** – Include your follower demographics, engagement statistics, past collaborations, and pricing.

- **Use Influencer Platforms** – Websites like AspireIQ, Upfluence, and Influencer.co connect influencers with brands.

Negotiating Your Worth

Many influencers undervalue their work. Here's how to negotiate effectively:

- **Know Your Value** – Your pricing should reflect engagement rates, audience size, content quality, and brand exclusivity.

- **Ask for Fair Compensation** – Don't accept free products unless it aligns with your goals. Set rates for posts, Stories, and Reels.

- **Clarify Deliverables** – Define content expectations, number of posts, and usage rights (e.g., whether the brand can repurpose your content).

- **Include Contract Terms** – Always work with clear contracts that outline payment terms, deadlines, and content guidelines.

---

4. Maintaining Authenticity in Brand Partnerships

One of the biggest challenges influencers face is maintaining authenticity while promoting brands. Here's how to ensure credibility:

Promote Products You Genuinely Like

Your audience trusts your recommendations, so only endorse products that align with your lifestyle and values.

Disclose Sponsored Content

Always use Instagram's **Paid Partnership** tool or include disclosures like #ad or #sponsored to comply with advertising laws.

Balance Sponsored and Organic Content

Avoid posting too many sponsored ads consecutively. Your feed should still feel natural and engaging.

Engage With Your Audience

Respond to questions about sponsored products honestly. If followers feel misled, it can damage your reputation.

---

5. Measuring Success and Improving Future Deals

To continue securing high-quality sponsorships, track and analyze your results.

Monitor Engagement Metrics

Brands look at performance metrics such as:

- Engagement Rate (likes, comments, shares, and saves)
- Click-Through Rate (CTR) (if promoting a website or product link)
- Conversion Rate (how many followers purchase through your affiliate link)

Gather Testimonials and Case Studies

If you deliver excellent results, brands may provide testimonials or repeat business. Compile these successes into your media kit.

Strengthen Future Negotiations

Analyze past collaborations to identify:

- Which type of content performed best?
- What pricing strategy worked best?

- Which brand relationships are worth continuing?

Conclusion

Sponsorships and brand deals on Instagram can be a rewarding income stream, but they require professionalism, strategic planning, and ethical responsibility. By building a strong personal brand, engaging authentically with your audience, and negotiating fair terms, you can establish long-term partnerships that benefit both you and the brands you work with. With the right approach, Instagram can become not just a platform for creativity but a profitable career opportunity.

CHAPTER V
Analytics and Optimization

6.1 Understanding Instagram Insights

6.1.1 Key Metrics to Track

Tracking key metrics on Instagram is essential for understanding how well your content is performing, what resonates with your audience, and how you can optimize your strategy for better engagement and growth. Instagram Insights provides a wealth of data, but knowing which metrics to focus on can make the difference between random posting and strategic success. Below are the key metrics every Instagram user—whether an individual creator, business, or influencer—should track.

1. Profile Metrics

Profile-level metrics give you an overview of your account's performance over time. These metrics help you understand how your overall presence is growing and whether your content strategy is effective.

- **Followers Count**: The total number of followers you have. A steady increase indicates audience growth, while fluctuations might signal content-related issues.

- **Follower Growth Rate**: The percentage increase or decrease in followers over a specific period. A healthy growth rate is more valuable than a high follower count alone.

- **Profile Visits**: The number of times people visit your profile. High profile visits mean your content is driving curiosity about your brand.

- **Website Clicks**: How many users click on the link in your bio. This is crucial for businesses and influencers driving traffic to external websites.

- **Email, Call, and Directions Clicks**: If you have a business account, Instagram tracks how often users engage with your contact buttons.

2. Content Performance Metrics

These metrics focus on the performance of individual posts, stories, reels, and videos. Understanding how your audience interacts with each piece of content allows you to refine your approach.

- **Reach**: The number of unique users who have seen your post. High reach means your content is being discovered by new audiences.

- **Impressions**: The total number of times your content is displayed. A high number of impressions compared to reach means people are viewing your content multiple times.

- **Engagement Rate**: This includes likes, comments, shares, and saves. A high engagement rate indicates that your content is resonating with your audience.

- **Shares**: The number of times your post has been shared via direct messages or stories. A high share count suggests strong content virality.

- **Saves**: The number of times users save your post for later. This is a good indicator of high-value content.

- **Comments**: Not just the count, but the quality of comments also matters. Thoughtful, longer comments indicate deeper audience engagement.

3. Instagram Stories Metrics

Stories are a powerful way to engage with your audience in real-time. Tracking how people interact with your stories helps you refine your strategy.

- **Story Views**: The total number of views on your story. Comparing this to your follower count helps gauge how many of your followers regularly engage with your stories.

- **Completion Rate**: The percentage of people who watched your entire story versus those who exited early. A low completion rate may indicate that your stories need to be more engaging.

- **Taps Forward/Backward**: Measures how users navigate through your story. Too many taps forward might mean your content is not engaging, while taps backward show users are interested in rewatching something.

- **Replies**: When people reply to your story, it signals engagement. This can be a great way to start direct conversations with your audience.

4. Instagram Reels Metrics

Reels have become a major growth driver on Instagram. Understanding these metrics will help you optimize your short-form video content.

- **Plays**: The number of times your reel was played, including multiple views by the same user.

- **Watch Time**: Average time users spend watching your reel. Higher watch time increases the likelihood of Instagram boosting your reel in the algorithm.

- **Shares & Saves**: Reels that get saved and shared frequently tend to go viral.

- **Engagement Rate**: The sum of likes, comments, shares, and saves divided by the total views. A high engagement rate indicates strong audience interest.

5. Instagram Live Metrics

Going live on Instagram can create real-time engagement with your audience. Monitoring live metrics helps you gauge how effective your live sessions are.

- **Live Viewers**: The number of unique users who watched your live video.

- **Peak Concurrent Viewers**: The highest number of viewers watching at one time.

- **Engagement During Live**: This includes comments, emoji reactions, and shares during the live session.

- **Replay Views**: If you save your live video, you can track how many people watch it later.

6. Audience Demographics and Behavior

Understanding who your audience is and how they behave on Instagram is crucial for tailoring content that appeals to them.

- **Follower Demographics**: Includes age, gender, and location. This data helps in personalizing content to match audience preferences.

- **Active Hours**: The times when your followers are most active. Posting at peak hours increases visibility.

- **Content Preferences**: By analyzing which types of posts (photos, carousels, reels, stories) get the most engagement, you can adjust your content strategy accordingly.

How to Use These Metrics for Optimization

Now that you know which metrics to track, here's how you can use them to improve your Instagram strategy:

1. **Identify High-Performing Content**: Analyze which posts, stories, and reels receive the highest engagement and replicate what works.

2. **Optimize Posting Times**: Use follower activity insights to post when your audience is most active.

3. **Adjust Content Strategy**: If certain content types (e.g., reels) consistently outperform others, allocate more effort toward them.

4. **Improve Engagement**: Respond to comments, encourage interactions, and create call-to-actions in captions to boost engagement.

5. **Test and Adapt**: Use A/B testing by posting similar content with slight variations (e.g., different hashtags, captions, or posting times) to see what works best.

6. **Monitor and Iterate**: Track these metrics regularly and adjust your strategy based on what the data shows.

By focusing on these key Instagram metrics and continuously refining your approach, you can build a strong presence, increase engagement, and grow your audience effectively.

6.1.2 Analyzing Post Performance

Understanding how your posts perform on Instagram is crucial for refining your content strategy and maximizing engagement. Instagram Insights provides a wealth of data that can help you determine what resonates with your audience, allowing you to adjust your approach accordingly. In this section, we will explore the key elements of post performance analysis, how to interpret the data, and actionable steps to improve your content strategy.

1. Key Metrics for Post Performance Analysis

When analyzing post performance, it is important to focus on key metrics that provide insights into engagement, reach, and overall effectiveness. Here are the main metrics you should monitor:

- **Impressions:** The total number of times your post has been displayed, regardless of whether it was clicked or engaged with.

- **Reach:** The number of unique accounts that have seen your post.

- **Engagement Rate:** The total interactions (likes, comments, shares, and saves) divided by the total reach, expressed as a percentage.

- **Likes:** The number of users who tapped the heart icon on your post.

- **Comments:** The number of user-generated responses under your post.

- **Shares:** The number of times your post has been shared via direct messages or stories.

- **Saves:** The number of users who saved your post for later viewing.

- **Profile Visits:** The number of times users viewed your profile after interacting with your post.

- **Follows:** The number of users who followed you after engaging with a specific post.

- **Click-Through Rate (CTR):** The percentage of users who clicked on your link (if applicable) after viewing the post.

By examining these metrics, you can gain a clear picture of how well your posts are performing and what aspects need improvement.

2. How to Access Instagram Insights for Posts

To access post analytics:

1. Open Instagram and navigate to your profile.

2. Tap on the post you want to analyze.

3. Click on **"View Insights"** below the post.

4. A detailed breakdown of engagement, reach, and impressions will be displayed.

If you have a Business or Creator account, you can access Instagram Insights for all your posts in one place:

- Go to your profile and tap the **menu (three horizontal lines)** in the top right corner.

- Select **Insights** and navigate to **Content You Shared** to view analytics for multiple posts at once.

3. Interpreting Post Performance Data

Analyzing your post performance involves looking at different data points and drawing conclusions about what works and what doesn't. Here are some strategies:

A. Understanding Engagement Trends

Engagement is a strong indicator of how well your audience connects with your content. If your engagement rate is high, it suggests that your audience finds value in your posts. To interpret engagement trends:

- Compare engagement rates across different types of posts (photos, videos, carousels, reels).

- Identify patterns in high-performing posts (e.g., topics, visuals, captions, hashtags).

- Look at the time and day when engagement peaks.

B. Identifying Content That Performs Best

Analyzing your top-performing posts can help you create more effective content. Ask yourself:

- What kind of images or videos received the most interactions?

- Were certain caption styles more engaging?

- Did posts with specific hashtags perform better?

- How did the length of the caption affect engagement?

C. Evaluating Reach vs. Engagement

A post with high reach but low engagement may indicate that while many people saw the content, they did not find it compelling enough to interact with. Possible reasons include:

- The post did not spark interest or curiosity.

- The caption was not engaging enough.

- The call-to-action (CTA) was weak or unclear.

Conversely, if a post has low reach but high engagement, it means your audience finds it valuable but it is not being widely distributed. In this case:

- Consider boosting the post using Instagram Ads.

- Encourage more shares and saves to increase reach.

D. Examining Hashtag and Location Tag Effectiveness

Hashtags and location tags can significantly impact post visibility. Use Instagram Insights to determine:

- Which hashtags brought the most reach and engagement.

- Whether location tagging increased impressions.

- If niche hashtags performed better than broad ones.

4. Improving Your Post Performance

Once you have analyzed your post performance, apply these strategies to optimize future content:

A. Optimize Posting Time

Using Instagram Insights, identify when your audience is most active and schedule posts accordingly. The best posting times typically depend on your specific audience but tend to be:

- Early mornings (7-9 AM) when people check their phones after waking up.

- Lunchtime (12-2 PM) when users browse social media during breaks.

- Evenings (6-9 PM) when people relax after work.

B. Experiment with Different Content Formats

If one type of content is underperforming, experiment with:

- **Carousel posts:** These often perform better than single-image posts due to multiple engagement opportunities.

- **Videos and reels:** Instagram's algorithm prioritizes video content.

- **User-generated content:** Encouraging followers to share their experiences with your brand.

C. Craft Compelling Captions

A strong caption can make a significant difference in engagement. To improve captions:

- Use storytelling to make posts more relatable.

- Include a clear CTA (e.g., "Tag a friend who needs to see this!").

- Ask questions to encourage comments.

D. Enhance Visual Appeal

High-quality visuals attract more engagement. Optimize your posts by:

- Using high-resolution images and well-edited videos.

- Maintaining a consistent aesthetic that aligns with your brand.

- Testing different color schemes and filters.

E. Leverage Instagram Stories and Reels

- Share your post in Stories to increase its visibility.

- Use interactive elements like polls, Q&A stickers, and countdowns.

- Repurpose high-performing posts into Reels for added exposure.

5. Tracking Progress Over Time

Post performance analysis should be an ongoing process. Create a tracking system:

- Use Instagram Insights to compare performance over weeks or months.

- Record key metrics in a spreadsheet to spot long-term trends.

- Adjust your strategy based on what consistently works.

Conclusion

Analyzing post performance is not just about tracking numbers; it is about understanding audience behavior and optimizing content accordingly. By regularly evaluating key metrics, refining your content strategy, and adapting to Instagram's evolving algorithms, you can significantly improve engagement, reach, and overall success on the platform.

6.1.3 Adjusting Your Strategy Based on Data

Understanding Instagram Insights is essential, but knowing how to leverage that data to refine and enhance your content strategy is what truly sets successful users apart. Once you have a clear grasp of key performance metrics and post analytics, you need to use that information to optimize your approach. This section will guide you through actionable steps to adjust your Instagram strategy based on data-driven insights.

1. Identifying Patterns and Trends

Data alone is meaningless unless you interpret it correctly. Look for recurring patterns in your analytics:

- **Engagement Trends**: Determine which types of posts (images, videos, carousels, reels) get the most engagement.

- **Best Posting Times**: Identify when your audience is most active and adjust your posting schedule accordingly.

- **Audience Demographics**: Understand who is engaging with your content (age, location, gender) to tailor your messaging.

- **Content Performance**: Compare the performance of different posts to identify which topics, styles, or formats resonate most.

Example: Suppose you analyze your insights and notice that your short-form video content (Reels) receives significantly more engagement than static image posts. Based on this, you decide to prioritize Reels in your content calendar while reducing the frequency of image posts.

2. Optimizing Your Content Strategy

Based on your analysis, tweak your content strategy to maximize impact:

- **Double Down on High-Performing Content**: If a particular type of content consistently performs well, create more of it.

- **Experiment with Underperforming Content**: Modify captions, visuals, or posting times for lower-performing posts to see if improvements can be made.

- **Incorporate User-Generated Content**: If you notice high engagement on posts featuring user-generated content, encourage more audience participation.

- **Refine Hashtag Strategy**: Use insights from past posts to determine which hashtags drive the most visibility and engagement.

Example: You notice that posts with long, storytelling-style captions receive more shares and comments than shorter captions. As a result, you start crafting longer, more engaging captions with calls to action that invite audience interaction.

3. Adjusting Posting Frequency and Timing

Regularly analyze your insights to determine the ideal frequency and timing for your posts:

- **Increase Posting Frequency**: If engagement is consistently high, experiment with increasing your posting schedule.

- **Optimize Posting Times**: If engagement fluctuates by day or time, adjust your schedule to post when your audience is most active.

- **Monitor Story and Reel Performance**: Instagram Stories and Reels have different algorithms—test various posting times and frequencies to maximize reach.

Example: After tracking your Insights for a month, you discover that posts published on Wednesday and Saturday evenings perform the best. You adjust your content calendar to prioritize these time slots for new uploads.

4. Enhancing Engagement Tactics

Your Instagram Insights can reveal how effectively you're engaging your audience. Improve engagement by:

- **Encouraging More Interaction**: Use interactive features such as polls, questions, and stickers in Stories.

- **Responding to Comments and DMs**: Engage with your audience promptly to foster a sense of community.

- **Collaborating with Influencers or Brands**: If certain collaborations drive higher engagement, explore similar partnerships.

- **Creating Call-to-Actions (CTAs)**: Encourage likes, comments, shares, and saves in your captions.

Example: You notice that posts with a direct question at the end of the caption receive significantly more comments. To leverage this, you start incorporating more open-ended questions and conversation starters in your posts.

5. Refining Paid Advertising Strategy

If you're using Instagram ads, Insights provide key data on ad performance. Adjust your ad strategy by:

- **Targeting the Right Audience**: Use demographic and engagement data to refine ad targeting.

- **Testing Different Ad Formats**: Compare carousel ads, story ads, and video ads to see which performs best.

- **Adjusting Ad Spend**: Allocate more budget to high-performing campaigns and pause or tweak underperforming ones.

Example: Your ad Insights reveal that video ads have a 30% higher engagement rate compared to static image ads. You decide to shift your budget towards producing and promoting more video content.

6. Monitoring and Adapting Over Time

Instagram trends and algorithms evolve, so continuous monitoring is crucial. Regularly:

- **Review Performance Reports**: Set aside time each week or month to analyze Instagram Insights.

- **Adjust Based on New Trends**: Stay updated with Instagram updates and trends to keep your strategy relevant.

- **Experiment and Iterate**: Try new strategies based on data and refine them over time.

Example: You notice a decline in engagement despite maintaining a consistent posting schedule. After analyzing your Insights, you realize that Instagram's algorithm has recently favored Reels over traditional posts. You pivot your strategy to include more Reels and interactive content to regain engagement.

Final Thoughts

Data-driven decision-making is key to Instagram success. By continually analyzing and adjusting your strategy based on Insights, you ensure that your content remains engaging, your audience stays interested, and your growth remains consistent. Leverage data, experiment with new approaches, and keep refining your strategy for optimal results.

6.2 Improving Your Content Strategy

6.2.1 Finding What Works for Your Audience

One of the most critical aspects of succeeding on Instagram is understanding what content resonates with your audience. Creating engaging content is not just about aesthetics; it is about delivering value, fostering interactions, and consistently analyzing performance to refine your approach. In this section, we will explore key strategies to determine what works best for your audience and how you can leverage data-driven insights to optimize your content strategy.

1. Understanding Your Audience

Before determining what content works best, you need to have a deep understanding of your target audience. Ask yourself the following questions:

- Who are they? (Age, gender, location, interests)

- What are their pain points or desires?

- When are they most active on Instagram?

- What type of content do they engage with the most? (Images, videos, carousels, reels, stories, etc.)

- What hashtags or trends do they follow?

You can gather these insights from Instagram Analytics (for business and creator accounts) or by manually observing interactions on your posts.

2. Leveraging Instagram Insights to Analyze Engagement

Instagram provides a powerful analytics tool called **Instagram Insights**, which allows you to monitor how your content is performing. Some of the key metrics to track include:

- **Reach**: The number of unique users who saw your content.

- **Impressions**: The total number of times your content was displayed.

- **Engagement Rate**: The total number of likes, comments, shares, and saves divided by the number of impressions.

- **Follower Growth**: How many new followers you gain over time.

- **Click-through Rate (CTR)**: If you use links in stories or ads, track how many users clicked on them.

By analyzing these metrics, you can identify patterns and trends regarding which types of content receive the most engagement.

---

3. Experimenting with Different Content Types

To find what works best, test different types of content and observe how your audience reacts. The main content formats on Instagram include:

A. Static Images

- Ideal for brand storytelling and visually appealing posts.

- Use high-quality visuals with engaging captions.

- Great for product showcases, quotes, and lifestyle images.

B. Carousels

- Allows users to swipe through multiple images or videos in a single post.

- Great for tutorials, step-by-step guides, before-and-after transformations, and detailed storytelling.

- Higher engagement rates compared to single-image posts.

C. Instagram Reels

- Short-form video content (up to 90 seconds) that is highly favored by Instagram's algorithm.

- Ideal for showcasing creativity, trends, educational content, or behind-the-scenes looks.

- Use popular sounds, trending challenges, and fast cuts to make your reels more engaging.

D. Instagram Stories

- Temporary content that disappears after 24 hours.
- Great for daily updates, Q&As, polls, behind-the-scenes clips, and engaging directly with followers.
- Interactive features such as stickers, polls, and countdowns help boost engagement.

E. Instagram Live

- Real-time streaming where you can interact with your audience instantly.
- Ideal for Q&A sessions, product launches, live tutorials, and interviews.
- Helps build trust and deeper engagement with your followers.

By experimenting with these formats, you can determine which ones resonate best with your audience.

4. A/B Testing for Content Performance

A/B testing involves posting two different versions of similar content and comparing their performance. Here's how you can conduct A/B testing effectively:

- Change only **one variable** at a time (e.g., caption, image, posting time, hashtags, or call-to-action).
- Post at the same time on different days to compare reach and engagement.
- Analyze the performance after 48 hours and adjust your future content strategy accordingly.

For example, you can test whether a carousel post gets more engagement than a single-image post, or whether a video with a certain type of background music performs better.

5. Studying Competitor and Industry Trends

Keeping an eye on competitors and industry trends can give you valuable insights into what content performs well. Here's how:

- Analyze your competitors' top-performing posts and engagement levels.

- Identify patterns in hashtags, post formats, and caption styles.

- Follow industry influencers and observe their content strategies.

- Stay updated with Instagram trends and algorithm changes.

6. Engaging with Your Audience

Audience engagement is not just about posting content—it's about building relationships. Here's how you can foster engagement:

- **Respond to comments and DMs:** Show your followers that you value their interactions.

- **Use interactive stickers in stories:** Polls, Q&As, and quizzes encourage participation.

- **Encourage user-generated content (UGC):** Ask followers to share photos or videos related to your brand.

- **Create community-driven content:** Feature customers, conduct shoutouts, or showcase fan art.

7. Optimizing Posting Time and Frequency

Posting at the right time and maintaining a consistent schedule can significantly impact engagement. Use Instagram Insights to determine when your audience is most active and schedule your posts accordingly.

General Posting Guidelines:

- Post at least **3-5 times per week** for optimal engagement.

- Use **stories daily** to stay connected with your audience.

- Experiment with different posting times and track engagement trends.

Conclusion

Finding what works for your audience requires a combination of **data analysis, content experimentation, and engagement strategies**. By leveraging Instagram Insights, experimenting with various content formats, studying industry trends, and engaging with your followers, you can create a content strategy that consistently drives growth and engagement. In the next section, we will explore how A/B testing can further refine your content performance and optimize your Instagram strategy.

6.2.2 A/B Testing for Better Results

Introduction to A/B Testing on Instagram

A/B testing, also known as split testing, is a powerful technique used to compare two versions of content to determine which one performs better. On Instagram, this involves testing different elements such as captions, images, hashtags, post timing, and formats to optimize engagement and growth.

A/B testing is essential for content creators, businesses, and influencers looking to refine their strategy based on data-driven insights. By systematically testing variations, you can identify what resonates most with your audience and continuously improve your content strategy.

Why A/B Testing Matters on Instagram

Instagram's algorithm prioritizes content that receives higher engagement, making A/B testing crucial for maximizing visibility and audience interaction. Some key benefits include:

- **Increased Engagement** – Discover what encourages likes, comments, and shares.

- **Optimized Posting Strategy** – Identify the best times and formats for posting.

- **Better Audience Understanding** – Learn what content your followers prefer.

- **Data-Driven Decision Making** – Eliminate guesswork and rely on real insights.

- **Improved Conversion Rates** – If you are monetizing your content, testing can lead to more sales and partnerships.

Elements You Can A/B Test on Instagram

To run successful A/B tests, you must determine which elements to compare. Here are the primary components:

1. Captions

- Test long vs. short captions.
- Experiment with different tones (formal vs. casual, humorous vs. informative).
- Try using a call-to-action (CTA) in one caption but not in another.

2. Images and Videos

- Compare different styles of images (e.g., product-focused vs. lifestyle-oriented).
- Test between static images and short videos.
- Use different color schemes and filters.

3. Hashtags

- Test different sets of hashtags.
- Experiment with the number of hashtags (e.g., 5 vs. 30 hashtags).
- Try niche hashtags vs. broad hashtags.

4. Post Timing

- Compare morning vs. evening posts.
- Test different days of the week.
- Analyze engagement rates based on time zones.

5. Post Format

- Compare Instagram Stories vs. Reels vs. feed posts.
- Test single images vs. carousel posts.
- Experiment with Instagram Live sessions.

6. Story Features

- Use polls, quizzes, and interactive stickers vs. plain stories.
- Test different text styles and sticker placements.

- Compare engagement on behind-the-scenes vs. promotional content.

How to Conduct an A/B Test on Instagram

A/B testing on Instagram requires a structured approach. Follow these steps:

Step 1: Define Your Goal

Before starting, identify what you want to improve. Examples include:

- Increasing likes and comments.
- Boosting follower growth.
- Improving link clicks from bio or Stories.
- Enhancing conversion rates for sales.

Step 2: Select One Variable to Test

For accurate results, test only one variable at a time. For instance, if you're testing captions, keep the image and posting time the same.

Step 3: Create Two Variations

Develop two slightly different versions of your content. For example:

- **Caption A:** "Excited for our new product launch! 🚀 #NewArrivals"
- **Caption B:** "Our latest product is here! 🎉 Click the link in bio to shop now! #ExclusiveDrop"

Step 4: Post at the Same Time

To ensure fair comparison, post both variations at the same time on different days or use Instagram Stories with different groups of followers.

Step 5: Analyze the Results

Wait at least 24-48 hours before comparing the performance metrics, including:

- Likes and comments.
- Shares and saves.

- Click-through rate (CTR) on links.

- Reach and impressions.

Step 6: Implement What Works Best

Use the data to refine your content strategy. If Caption B performed better, use similar CTAs and wording in future posts.

Best Practices for A/B Testing on Instagram

- **Keep Tests Simple** – Testing too many variables at once can lead to inconclusive results.

- **Be Patient** – Give each test enough time to gather meaningful insights.

- **Use Instagram Insights** – Leverage analytics to track engagement and performance.

- **Document Findings** – Maintain a record of what works best to refine your long-term strategy.

Tools to Enhance A/B Testing on Instagram

Several tools can assist with A/B testing and performance tracking:

- **Instagram Insights** – Built-in analytics for business and creator accounts.

- **Later** – A social media scheduling tool that provides engagement reports.

- **Hootsuite** – Allows tracking and comparing post-performance.

- **Sprout Social** – Advanced analytics and engagement insights.

Conclusion

A/B testing is a game-changer for optimizing Instagram content. By experimenting with different variables and analyzing performance metrics, you can refine your strategy, boost engagement, and achieve your Instagram goals. Consistently testing and adapting ensures you stay ahead in the ever-evolving Instagram landscape.

6.2.3 Consistency and Content Scheduling

One of the most important aspects of a successful Instagram strategy is maintaining consistency. Posting regularly not only keeps your audience engaged but also signals to the Instagram algorithm that you are an active user, increasing your visibility. However, consistency does not mean posting randomly; it involves careful planning and scheduling to maximize impact. This section will cover why consistency matters, how to determine the best posting frequency, and the tools and strategies you can use to maintain a consistent content schedule.

The Importance of Consistency

Consistency in posting helps build trust with your audience. If your followers know when to expect new content, they are more likely to engage with your posts. Additionally, regular posting increases your chances of being featured in the Explore tab and on your followers' feeds. Here are key benefits of consistency:

1. **Improved Engagement Rates** - Accounts that post consistently tend to receive more likes, comments, and shares compared to those that post sporadically.

2. **Better Brand Recall** - Posting regularly ensures that your audience remembers you, reinforcing your brand presence.

3. **Higher Algorithm Favorability** - Instagram's algorithm favors active users. The more consistently you post, the better your chances of being shown to a larger audience.

4. **Stronger Community Building** - Engaging consistently allows you to build and nurture relationships with your followers, turning them into loyal fans.

Finding the Right Posting Frequency

There is no universal rule for how often you should post, as it depends on your niche, audience, and goals. However, here are some general guidelines:

- **Personal Accounts:** 3-4 times per week

- **Business or Brand Accounts:** 4-7 times per week

- **Influencers & Content Creators:** Daily posts and frequent Stories/Reels

Factors to Consider When Setting Your Posting Frequency:

- **Audience Behavior:** Use Instagram Insights to analyze when your followers are most active.

- **Content Quality:** It is better to post high-quality content less frequently than to post low-quality content every day.

- **Time and Resources:** Ensure you can consistently create and post content without burnout.

Best Times to Post on Instagram

Determining the best times to post requires analyzing your audience's habits. However, studies suggest the following time frames for optimal engagement:

- **Weekdays:** 6 AM - 8 AM (morning engagement), 11 AM - 1 PM (lunch break), 6 PM - 9 PM (evening relaxation)

- **Weekends:** 10 AM - 12 PM is generally the best window for Saturday and Sunday

Using **Instagram Insights**, you can track your audience's peak activity and adjust your posting schedule accordingly.

Creating a Content Calendar

A **content calendar** is essential for organizing and scheduling posts in advance. It helps you:

- Plan content around important dates, trends, and events.

- Maintain a balanced mix of content types (photos, videos, Stories, Reels, etc.).

- Avoid last-minute stress and rushed posts.

Steps to Create a Content Calendar:

1. **Define Your Goals** - Identify whether you aim for engagement, brand awareness, sales, or community building.

2. **Choose Your Content Themes** - Select a mix of educational, entertaining, and promotional content.

3. **Decide Posting Days and Times** - Based on your audience data, choose the best posting schedule.

4. **Prepare and Organize Content in Advance** - Have visuals and captions ready for future posts.

5. **Use Scheduling Tools** - Automate your posting schedule using tools like Later, Buffer, or Hootsuite.

Tools for Scheduling Instagram Posts

To maintain consistency without constantly being online, leverage scheduling tools that allow you to pre-plan and automate posts. Here are some top tools:

- **Meta Business Suite** (formerly Facebook Creator Studio) – Free and allows direct scheduling for Instagram.

- **Later** – Offers a visual content planner, ideal for managing feed aesthetics.

- **Hootsuite** – Allows scheduling, analytics tracking, and team collaboration.

- **Buffer** – Simplified scheduling with analytics and engagement tracking.

- **Planoly** – Designed for Instagram, includes drag-and-drop content calendar.

Tips for Maintaining Consistency

1. **Batch Create Content** - Dedicate specific days to creating and editing multiple posts at once.

2. **Set Reminders** - Use notifications or alarms to remind you of important posting times.

3. **Engage Regularly** - Consistency is not just about posting but also interacting with followers through comments, DMs, and Stories.

4. **Analyze and Adjust** - Regularly check your performance metrics and refine your schedule for better results.

5. **Stay Flexible** - While consistency is key, be open to adjusting based on audience feedback and trends.

Final Thoughts

Consistency in posting is one of the strongest factors in growing an Instagram presence. By understanding your audience's behavior, planning ahead, and using scheduling tools, you can maintain a steady and engaging content flow without feeling overwhelmed. Mastering this strategy will help boost engagement, enhance brand recall, and ultimately lead to a more successful Instagram presence.

CHAPTER VI
Monetizing Instagram

7.1 Earning Money Through Instagram

7.1.1 Different Ways to Monetize Your Account

Instagram has evolved far beyond just a photo-sharing app; it has become a lucrative platform where creators, influencers, and businesses can generate income in multiple ways. Whether you are a content creator, an entrepreneur, or someone looking to build a side hustle, Instagram offers numerous monetization opportunities. Below, we will explore the most effective ways to earn money on Instagram.

1. Brand Sponsorships and Influencer Marketing

One of the most popular ways to make money on Instagram is through brand partnerships. Companies are willing to pay influencers with engaged followings to promote their products or services.

How It Works:

- Brands collaborate with Instagram users who align with their target audience.
- Influencers create posts, stories, reels, or IGTV videos featuring the brand's products.
- The partnership can be a one-time deal or an ongoing sponsorship.

How to Get Brand Deals:

- **Grow Your Audience:** Brands look for influencers with active and engaged followers.
- **Pick a Niche:** Specializing in a niche (e.g., fashion, fitness, tech) helps attract the right brands.

- **Use Hashtags and Geotags:** This increases discoverability for potential brand collaborations.

- **Reach Out to Brands:** Send direct messages or emails to brands you want to work with.

- **Sign Up for Influencer Marketplaces:** Platforms like AspireIQ, Upfluence, and BrandSnob connect influencers with brands.

How Much Can You Earn?

- Influencers with 10k-50k followers can earn anywhere from $100 to $500 per post.

- Those with 100k+ followers can charge $1,000 or more per sponsored post.

- Mega-influencers with over a million followers can demand tens of thousands of dollars per post.

2. Affiliate Marketing

Affiliate marketing allows Instagram users to earn a commission by promoting other companies' products and driving sales.

How It Works:

- Sign up for affiliate programs (e.g., Amazon Associates, ShareASale, Rakuten, or brand-specific programs).

- Receive unique tracking links or discount codes.

- Promote products in posts, stories, and reels.

- Earn a commission when someone makes a purchase using your link or code.

Best Practices for Affiliate Marketing:

- **Promote Products You Believe In:** Your audience will trust your recommendations if they feel authentic.

- **Use Instagram Stories:** Features like swipe-up links (for accounts with 10k+ followers) or link stickers help drive traffic.

- **Create Product Reviews and Tutorials:** These encourage engagement and conversions.

- **Track Your Performance:** Use affiliate dashboards to analyze what works best.

Potential Earnings:

- Commissions range from 5% to 50%, depending on the product and affiliate program.

- Some influencers make $500 to $10,000+ per month through affiliate marketing alone.

3. Selling Your Own Products or Services

Many Instagram users monetize their accounts by launching their own businesses, whether it's selling physical products, digital goods, or offering services.

How It Works:

- **Physical Products:** Clothing, accessories, handmade crafts, artwork, or any tangible product.

- **Digital Products:** E-books, online courses, templates, stock photos, or presets.

- **Services:** Coaching, consulting, fitness training, photography, or social media management.

How to Sell on Instagram:

- **Use Instagram Shopping:** Tag products in posts and stories for direct purchases.

- **Leverage Instagram Live:** Showcase your products and answer customer questions in real-time.

- **Create a Business Profile:** Gain access to analytics and ad tools.

- **Run Promotions and Giveaways:** Engage your audience and attract new customers.

Earnings Potential:

- Depends on pricing and demand.

- Some small business owners generate six to seven figures solely through Instagram sales.

4. Offering Exclusive Content Through Subscriptions

Instagram has introduced monetization tools such as Subscriptions, where creators can charge followers for exclusive content.

How It Works:

- Users pay a monthly fee to access subscriber-only content.

- Creators offer premium content, such as behind-the-scenes footage, tutorials, or special Q&A sessions.

Best Strategies for Success:

- **Provide Valuable Content:** Exclusive tips, live sessions, and early access to content.

- **Promote Your Subscription:** Use Instagram posts and stories to highlight the benefits.

- **Engage With Subscribers:** Make them feel valued by responding to comments and DMs.

Earnings Potential:

- Subscription fees range from $0.99 to $99.99 per month per user.

- Earnings depend on the number of subscribers and retention rate.

5. Instagram Live Badges & Donations

Instagram Live Badges allow followers to support their favorite creators by purchasing virtual badges during live streams.

How It Works:

- Viewers buy badges ($0.99, $1.99, or $4.99) while watching live videos.

- Creators receive a portion of the revenue from Instagram.

Tips for Maximizing Earnings:

- **Host Regular Live Sessions:** Engage with your audience consistently.

- **Encourage Donations:** Mention the badge feature during your live streams.
- **Offer Incentives:** Give a shout-out to badge supporters.

Earnings Potential:

- Depending on audience engagement, some creators make $100 to $5,000+ per live session.

6. Instagram Ad Revenue (IGTV Ads and Reels Bonus Programs)

Instagram provides ad revenue-sharing opportunities through IGTV ads and Reels Play Bonus Programs.

How It Works:

- Creators enable ads on their IGTV videos.
- Reels Play Bonus pays eligible users based on the performance of their Reels.

How to Qualify:

- Have an Instagram Creator or Business account.
- Meet Instagram's monetization policies.
- Consistently create high-quality video content.

Earnings Potential:

- IGTV ad revenue shares 55% with creators.
- Reels Play Bonus varies but can reach thousands per month for viral creators.

Final Thoughts

Monetizing an Instagram account requires strategy, patience, and consistency. While there are multiple ways to generate income, success depends on building an engaged audience, providing valuable content, and leveraging Instagram's monetization tools effectively. Whether you choose brand sponsorships, affiliate marketing, selling your own products, or using Instagram's built-in monetization features, there are endless opportunities to turn your Instagram presence into a profitable venture.

By implementing these strategies, you can start generating income and transform your Instagram account from a simple social media profile into a thriving business platform.

7.1.2 Instagram Affiliate Marketing

Introduction to Instagram Affiliate Marketing

Affiliate marketing is one of the most effective ways to earn money through Instagram without creating or selling your own products. By promoting products or services from brands and earning a commission on each sale made through your unique affiliate link, you can generate a steady stream of income. Instagram's visual nature and engaged user base make it an ideal platform for affiliate marketing.

In this section, we will explore how Instagram affiliate marketing works, how to find the right affiliate programs, strategies for maximizing your earnings, and tips for long-term success.

How Instagram Affiliate Marketing Works

Instagram affiliate marketing involves a few key steps:

1. **Joining an Affiliate Program:** You need to partner with a company or platform that offers an affiliate program.

2. **Getting a Unique Affiliate Link:** After joining, you receive a unique tracking link that allows the company to track sales attributed to you.

3. **Promoting Affiliate Products:** You create content featuring the product and share your affiliate link.

4. **Earning Commissions:** You receive a commission for every sale made through your link.

Instagram does not currently support clickable links in post captions, so affiliates use methods like link-in-bio tools, Stories with swipe-up links (if eligible), and Instagram Shops to direct users to their affiliate links.

Finding the Right Affiliate Programs

Choosing the right affiliate program is crucial to success. Here are some factors to consider:

- **Relevance to Your Audience:** Promote products that align with your niche and followers' interests.

- **Commission Structure:** Look for programs that offer competitive commissions (e.g., 10-30% per sale).

- **Cookie Duration:** The longer the cookie duration (e.g., 30-90 days), the higher your chances of earning commissions.

- **Credibility of the Brand:** Partner with reputable brands that have a positive reputation and high conversion rates.

Popular Affiliate Networks and Programs

Many brands and companies offer affiliate programs. Some of the best affiliate networks include:

- **Amazon Associates:** Ideal for a wide range of products.

- **ShareASale:** Offers thousands of merchants across various industries.

- **CJ Affiliate (Commission Junction):** Connects affiliates with well-known brands.

- **Rakuten Advertising:** Provides opportunities with premium brands.

- **Impact:** Offers partnerships with top companies.

- **LTK (LikeToKnowIt):** Popular among fashion and lifestyle influencers.

How to Promote Affiliate Products on Instagram

There are multiple ways to share affiliate links and increase your sales:

1. Instagram Stories and Highlights

- If you have over 10,000 followers or a verified account, you can use the **Swipe-Up feature** to add direct affiliate links.

- Save key affiliate promotions to **Story Highlights** for ongoing exposure.

2. Link in Bio

- Use bio link tools like **Linktree, Beacons, or Later's Linkin.bio** to display multiple affiliate links.

- Regularly update your bio with the latest promotions.

3. Feed Posts and Carousel Posts

- Create **high-quality lifestyle photos** featuring the product.
- Use captions to tell a story and include a CTA like "Link in bio for details!"
- Carousels allow multiple images to showcase product features.

4. Instagram Reels and Video Content

- Demonstrate how to use the product in a **short, engaging video**.
- Add trending music and hashtags to increase reach.
- Mention the affiliate link location (e.g., "Check my bio for the link!").

5. IGTV and Instagram Live

- Provide in-depth reviews or tutorials on IGTV.
- Host **live Q&A sessions** to answer audience questions about the product.
- Pin a comment with your affiliate link during live sessions.

Optimizing for Maximum Conversions

To maximize your affiliate earnings, follow these best practices:

1. Be Authentic and Transparent

- Share **genuine experiences** with the product.
- Disclose affiliate partnerships clearly using **#ad** or **#affiliate**.

2. Create High-Quality Content

- Use **bright, well-composed images** to grab attention.
- **Write compelling captions** that highlight the product's benefits.

3. Use Effective Calls-to-Action (CTAs)

- Example CTAs:

- o "Click the link in my bio for a special discount!"
- o "Swipe up to grab this limited-time offer!"
- o "DM me for my exclusive promo code!"

4. Engage With Your Audience

- Reply to comments and DMs about the product.
- Host giveaways to boost engagement and trust.

5. Track Performance and Adjust Strategies

- Use affiliate dashboards to monitor **clicks, conversions, and earnings**.
- Experiment with different content formats to see what resonates best.

Common Mistakes to Avoid

Many beginners make mistakes that hinder their affiliate marketing success. Here's what to watch out for:

- **Promoting too many unrelated products** – Stay within your niche.
- **Not disclosing affiliate links** – Instagram's policies require transparency.
- **Using low-quality images or spammy captions** – Focus on professional-looking content.
- **Not engaging with followers** – Building trust leads to more conversions.

The Future of Instagram Affiliate Marketing

Instagram is continuously evolving, with new features like **Instagram's Native Affiliate Program**, which allows influencers to tag products and earn commissions directly from Instagram. This could simplify the affiliate process and provide better tracking.

Final Thoughts

Instagram affiliate marketing is a lucrative way to monetize your content while providing value to your audience. By choosing the right affiliate programs, creating high-quality content, and engaging with your followers, you can build a sustainable income stream.

Consistency, authenticity, and strategic promotion are the keys to long-term success in affiliate marketing. Start small, experiment with different strategies, and refine your approach based on performance data to maximize your earnings.

7.1.3 Selling Your Own Products or Services

Instagram has evolved from a simple photo-sharing platform into a powerful e-commerce tool. With over a billion active users, it provides entrepreneurs and businesses with a unique opportunity to showcase their products and services to a global audience. Whether you are selling handmade crafts, digital products, coaching services, or physical goods, Instagram offers numerous features to help you connect with potential buyers and drive sales. In this section, we will explore how to set up your business on Instagram, optimize your profile for sales, and implement strategies to increase revenue.

1. Setting Up Your Business for Sales on Instagram

Switch to a Business or Creator Account

Before selling on Instagram, it is essential to switch your personal profile to a Business or Creator account. This allows access to Instagram Insights, advertising tools, and the ability to add contact buttons. To switch:

- Go to your profile and tap the menu (three horizontal lines).

- Select **Settings** > **Account** > **Switch to Professional Account**.

- Choose either a **Business** or **Creator** account based on your needs.

- Add relevant business details such as category, contact information, and website.

Optimize Your Instagram Bio for Sales

Your bio is the first impression potential customers get, so it should be clear and compelling. Include:

- A short, engaging description of what you offer.

- A call-to-action (e.g., "Shop Now!" or "DM for Orders").

- A link to your online store, website, or product catalog (using Linktree or Instagram's link feature).

2. Using Instagram Shopping Features

Setting Up Instagram Shop

Instagram Shopping allows you to tag products in posts and Stories, creating a seamless shopping experience. To enable this feature:

1. Ensure you meet Instagram's **Commerce Eligibility Requirements**.

2. Connect your account to a **Facebook Shop** or an **approved e-commerce platform** (like Shopify or BigCommerce).

3. Upload your product catalog via **Facebook Business Manager**.

4. Enable **Shopping** in Instagram settings and submit your account for review.

5. Once approved, tag products in posts, Reels, and Stories to make them shoppable.

Using Product Tags and Stickers

Instagram allows businesses to tag products directly in images and videos. Best practices include:

- **Using clear, high-quality images** to showcase your products.

- **Tagging multiple products** in a single post to encourage bulk purchases.

- **Using Shopping Stickers** in Stories for real-time promotions.

3. Creating Engaging Content to Drive Sales

Posting High-Quality Product Photos and Videos

Instagram is a visual platform, so high-quality images and videos are essential. Best practices include:

- Using **natural lighting** to enhance product visibility.

- Taking multiple **angles and close-ups** for better product representation.

- Using **carousel posts** to showcase product variations and features.

- Posting short **video demonstrations** or testimonials.

Leveraging Reels for Promotions

Reels offer a dynamic way to showcase products. Consider:

- **Behind-the-scenes content** to build authenticity.

- **Tutorials and how-to videos** demonstrating product use.

- **Before-and-after transformations** for services like beauty, fitness, or home improvement.

Writing Compelling Captions

Captions should be engaging, informative, and encourage action. A good caption format includes:

- **A hook** (Grab attention with a question or bold statement).

- **Value proposition** (Highlight benefits of your product/service).

- **Call-to-action (CTA)** (Encourage users to "Shop Now," "DM for orders," or "Click the link in bio").

---

4. Using Instagram Stories and Live to Sell

Selling Through Instagram Stories

Stories disappear after 24 hours, making them perfect for limited-time promotions. Use:

- Polls and Q&A stickers to gauge customer interest.

- Countdown stickers for product launches or sales.

- Swipe-up links (for accounts with 10K+ followers) to direct users to your store.

Hosting Instagram Live Shopping Events

Live shopping allows real-time interaction with customers. Strategies include:

- Product demonstrations and Q&A sessions.

- Exclusive discounts for viewers.
- Guest appearances from influencers or satisfied customers.

5. Implementing Effective Sales Strategies

Running Promotions and Discounts

Offering discounts can drive urgency and boost sales. Popular methods include:

- Limited-time flash sales.
- Bundle deals (Buy one, get one free).
- Exclusive discounts for Instagram followers.

Influencer and User-Generated Content (UGC)

Leverage influencers and customers to promote your products:

- Send free products to influencers for review.
- Encourage customers to tag your brand in their posts.
- Repost user-generated content to build trust and social proof.

6. Managing Orders and Customer Service

Handling Orders Efficiently

If you sell physical products, ensure smooth order processing:

- Use e-commerce platforms like Shopify, Etsy, or WooCommerce for automation.
- Provide clear shipping and return policies.
- Send order confirmation and tracking updates.

Providing Excellent Customer Support

Customer satisfaction drives repeat sales. Best practices include:

- Responding to DMs and comments promptly.

- Offering multiple contact methods (WhatsApp, email, or chatbots).

- Handling complaints professionally and offering refunds when necessary.

7. Measuring Success and Scaling Your Business

Tracking Key Performance Metrics

Use Instagram Insights to measure:

- Engagement rate (likes, comments, shares).

- Conversion rate (how many users turn into customers).

- Best-performing content to refine strategy.

Scaling Your Instagram Business

Once sales pick up, consider:

- Expanding to other platforms (Facebook Marketplace, TikTok Shop).

- Investing in Instagram Ads to reach a wider audience.

- Outsourcing tasks like content creation or order fulfillment.

Final Thoughts

Selling on Instagram requires consistency, creativity, and strategic planning. By optimizing your profile, leveraging Instagram's shopping features, creating engaging content, and providing excellent customer service, you can turn your Instagram account into a thriving business. Start implementing these strategies today and watch your sales grow!

7.2 Working with Brands and Sponsorships

7.2.1 How to Get Brand Deals

Introduction

Brand deals are one of the most lucrative ways to monetize your Instagram presence. Whether you're a micro-influencer or a well-established content creator, partnering with brands can help you generate income while promoting products or services you genuinely support. However, securing brand deals requires strategy, consistency, and a well-crafted personal brand. In this section, we will explore how to get brand deals, from building a compelling profile to pitching to brands effectively.

Understanding Brand Partnerships

A brand deal is a collaboration between an influencer and a company where the influencer promotes a product or service in exchange for compensation. This can take various forms, including:

- **Sponsored posts** – Creating content featuring the brand's product or service.

- **Affiliate marketing** – Earning a commission for every sale made through your unique link.

- **Brand ambassadorships** – Long-term partnerships where influencers represent a brand over an extended period.

- **Giveaways and contests** – Collaborating with brands to promote their products through engagement-driven campaigns.

Step 1: Build a Strong Personal Brand

Before brands consider working with you, they need to see a strong and consistent personal brand. Here's how to establish one:

Define Your Niche

Brands prefer influencers who have a clear niche and a loyal audience. Choose a niche that aligns with your interests and expertise, such as:

- Fashion

- Fitness

- Beauty and skincare

- Technology

- Travel

- Food and lifestyle

Optimize Your Instagram Profile

Your profile should clearly communicate your brand identity and value. Ensure you:

- Have a professional and engaging bio.

- Use a high-quality profile picture.

- Include a business email for collaboration inquiries.

- Highlight your best work using Instagram Highlights.

Create High-Quality Content

Your content should be visually appealing, informative, and engaging. Brands look for influencers who:

- Maintain a consistent aesthetic.

- Post high-resolution images and videos.

- Use captions that encourage engagement.

- Utilize Instagram features like Reels, Stories, and IGTV.

Step 2: Grow Your Audience and Engagement

Brands are not just looking at follower count—they prioritize engagement and influence. Here's how to grow your audience effectively:

Engage With Your Followers

- Respond to comments and direct messages.

- Use interactive features like polls, Q&A, and quizzes in Stories.

- Collaborate with other influencers for cross-promotion.

Use Relevant Hashtags and Geotags

- Research trending hashtags within your niche.

- Use a mix of popular and niche-specific hashtags.

- Geotag posts to attract local engagement.

Post Consistently

- Create a content calendar to maintain a regular posting schedule.

- Experiment with posting times to see when your audience is most active.

- Balance promotional content with organic, value-driven posts.

Step 3: Build Relationships With Brands

Identify Brands That Align With Your Values

Work with brands that match your niche and values. Conduct research by:

- Looking at brands other influencers in your niche work with.

- Checking brands' Instagram pages for collaboration announcements.

- Exploring influencer marketing platforms like AspireIQ, Upfluence, and BrandSnob.

Engage With Brands Organically

- Follow their Instagram accounts.

- Like, comment, and share their posts.

- Mention them in your content when relevant (without tagging them excessively).

Get Listed on Influencer Platforms

Many brands use influencer marketing platforms to find collaborators. Sign up for platforms such as:

- **FameBit**

- **Grapevine**

- **TRIBE**

- **Heepsy**

- **Influence.co**

Step 4: Craft the Perfect Pitch

Once you have built a strong profile and engaged with potential brand partners, the next step is reaching out. Here's how to craft an effective pitch:

Find the Right Contact

Look for brand representatives in marketing or influencer outreach. You can find them:

- On the brand's Instagram bio (business email).

- Through LinkedIn searches.

- On the brand's website (press or media section).

Write a Compelling Email or DM

A good pitch includes:

- A personalized greeting.

- A brief introduction about who you are and your niche.

- A statement on why you love the brand.

- Data-driven insights about your audience and engagement rate.

- Examples of past collaborations (if applicable).

- A clear call-to-action, such as requesting a meeting or offering content ideas.

Sample Pitch Email:

Subject: Collaboration Opportunity with [Your Instagram Handle]

Dear [Brand Representative's Name],

I'm [Your Name], a [Your Niche] content creator with [Number] engaged followers on Instagram. I've been a fan of [Brand Name] and love how your products align with my audience's interests in [Your Niche].

I would love to collaborate and introduce your brand to my followers through authentic and engaging content. Here are some of my audience insights:

- Average engagement rate: [Percentage]%

- Primary audience: [Demographics]

- Successful past collaborations: [Mention any relevant brands]

I'd love to discuss how we can create a partnership that provides value to both my audience and your brand. Let me know if we can schedule a time to chat further!

Best regards,
[Your Name]
[Your Instagram Handle]
[Your Contact Information]

Step 5: Negotiate Your Rates

Once a brand responds positively, be prepared to discuss pricing. Key points include:

- Your standard rates for sponsored posts, Stories, and Reels.

- Additional costs for exclusivity or additional content.

- Deliverables and deadlines.

Factors That Affect Your Rates:

- Follower count and engagement rate.

- Industry/niche competition.

- Content quality and production effort.

- Usage rights (e.g., whether the brand can repurpose your content).

Conclusion

Getting brand deals on Instagram requires dedication, authenticity, and strategic networking. By building a compelling personal brand, engaging with your audience, and effectively pitching to brands, you can successfully secure lucrative brand partnerships. The key is to remain professional, deliver high-quality content, and maintain long-term relationships with brands that align with your values.

Are you ready to start pitching to brands? Begin implementing these strategies today, and watch your Instagram collaborations grow!

7.2.2 Negotiating Your Rates

When working with brands and securing sponsorships on Instagram, one of the most crucial aspects is negotiating your rates effectively. Whether you're an aspiring influencer or an established creator, knowing how to set your pricing, communicate your value, and negotiate terms can significantly impact your earning potential. In this section, we will explore strategies for determining your worth, understanding industry standards, and confidently negotiating fair compensation for your work.

Understanding Your Value

Before entering negotiations, it's essential to assess your value as an influencer. Brands look at multiple factors when deciding how much to pay influencers, including:

- **Follower Count**: While follower numbers matter, engagement rate and content quality often hold more weight.

- **Engagement Rate**: A highly engaged audience (likes, comments, shares, and saves) indicates strong influence and justifies higher rates.

- **Content Quality**: Professional, high-quality visuals and compelling captions make your content more appealing to brands.

- **Audience Demographics**: Brands pay more for influencers whose followers align with their target market.

- **Niche and Industry**: Some industries (fashion, beauty, finance, and tech) have higher budgets for influencer marketing than others.

- **Past Collaborations**: If you have worked with reputable brands, you can leverage that experience to negotiate better rates.

Setting Your Pricing

To negotiate effectively, you must first set a pricing structure based on your content deliverables and industry standards. Common pricing models include:

1. Fixed Pricing per Post

- Instagram Post: $100 - $10,000+ (depending on influencer size and engagement)

- Instagram Story (per frame): $50 - $3,000+

- Instagram Reel: $250 - $15,000+

- Carousel Post: Typically higher than a single post due to increased exposure

2. Package Deals

Many influencers offer bundled services for brands, such as:

- A single Instagram post + 3 stories

- A dedicated Reel + one carousel post

- Monthly partnerships for continuous exposure

3. Performance-Based Pricing

If a brand is hesitant about upfront costs, consider negotiating a commission-based deal where you earn a percentage of sales generated through your content (affiliate marketing).

4. Usage Rights and Exclusivity Fees

Brands often request additional usage rights for repurposing your content. Be sure to charge extra for:

- **Content Licensing**: If the brand wants to use your post for ads, set a licensing fee.

- **Exclusivity Agreements**: If the brand requires you not to work with competitors, charge an exclusivity fee based on the duration of the agreement.

Negotiation Strategies

Once you establish your baseline rates, it's time to negotiate with confidence. Here's how:

1. Research the Brand's Budget

Larger brands usually have bigger marketing budgets, while smaller businesses may have limited funds. Research their past influencer partnerships to gauge how much they typically pay.

2. Start Higher Than Your Minimum

Always quote a price slightly above your target rate to leave room for negotiation. For example, if you want to earn $500 per post, you might quote $700, allowing the brand to counteroffer.

3. Showcase Your ROI (Return on Investment)

Brands care about results. Highlight your engagement rates, past campaign successes, and conversion metrics. For instance:

- "My average story views are 20,000+, and I've driven 5% click-through rates on past brand promotions."

- "In my last sponsored post, my audience generated 500+ website visits for a brand."

4. Offer Additional Value

Instead of lowering your rate, propose added value such as:

- An extra story mention
- A behind-the-scenes Reel
- Extended promotion on other platforms (YouTube, TikTok, blog, etc.)

5. Be Ready to Walk Away

If a brand offers significantly lower than your worth, don't hesitate to decline politely. Sticking to your rates helps maintain industry standards and avoids undervaluing your work.

6. Get Everything in Writing

Once you agree on terms, request a written contract outlining:

- Payment amount and schedule
- Deliverables (post format, number of posts, captions, etc.)
- Content approval process
- Usage rights and exclusivity clauses

Handling Common Objections

During negotiations, brands may push back on your rates. Here's how to respond:

- **"We don't have the budget for that."** → "I understand! I can adjust the deliverables or offer a package that fits your budget while ensuring quality engagement."
- **"Other influencers charge less."** → "I appreciate that! My pricing reflects my engagement rate, content quality, and past successful brand collaborations."
- **"Can you post for free in exchange for exposure?"** → "I value collaborations, but I have invested time and resources into building my audience. I'd love to discuss a fair partnership."

Final Thoughts

Negotiating your rates as an Instagram influencer is both an art and a skill. By knowing your worth, setting clear pricing structures, and confidently handling negotiations, you can ensure fair compensation for your work. Remember, successful collaborations are about mutual value—brands gain exposure, and you get paid for your creativity and influence.

Always stay professional, be flexible when necessary, and never undervalue your hard work. The more experience you gain, the stronger your negotiation skills will become, leading to higher earnings and long-term brand partnerships.

7.2.3 Delivering Value to Brands

Working with brands on Instagram is not just about securing deals; it's about building long-term partnerships that bring mutual benefit. Brands are looking for influencers and content creators who can drive engagement, boost brand awareness, and ultimately increase conversions. To maintain successful collaborations, you need to demonstrate the value you bring to the table. This chapter will explore key strategies to deliver value to brands effectively.

Understanding What Brands Look For

Before approaching a brand or negotiating a deal, it's crucial to understand what they value in a partnership. Brands typically look for:

- **Authenticity** – A creator who aligns with their brand values and has a genuine connection with their audience.

- **Engagement Rates** – High interaction levels through likes, comments, and shares.

- **Quality Content** – Professional-looking images, videos, and well-written captions.

- **Audience Demographics** – Followers that match their target market.

- **Conversion Ability** – The capability to drive website traffic, sales, or sign-ups.

Understanding these factors will help you craft content and campaigns that resonate with both the brand and your audience.

Creating High-Quality, Brand-Aligned Content

To deliver real value to brands, your content should seamlessly integrate their products or services while maintaining your unique style. Here's how to do it:

1. Maintain Authenticity

Brands prefer influencers who showcase their products naturally. Forced endorsements can lead to low engagement and reduced trust among followers. Ensure that:

- The product aligns with your lifestyle and audience.
- You create content in a way that feels natural and organic.
- Your captions reflect genuine personal experiences with the brand.

2. Leverage Storytelling

Instead of just showcasing a product, tell a compelling story around it. Use:

- Personal anecdotes about how the product fits into your life.
- Problem-solving narratives that highlight how the brand helps overcome challenges.
- Behind-the-scenes content showcasing the making of the post.

3. Use High-Quality Visuals

Your Instagram feed is your portfolio. To attract and retain brand deals, ensure:

- Your photos and videos are well-lit, clear, and aesthetically pleasing.
- You use a consistent editing style that aligns with the brand.
- You experiment with various formats, such as carousel posts, Reels, and Stories, to enhance engagement.

Engaging Your Audience Effectively

Brands invest in creators who can generate meaningful engagement. To boost audience interaction:

1. Encourage User Interaction

- Ask engaging questions in captions.

- Use polls, quizzes, and stickers in Stories to increase participation.

- Prompt followers to share their thoughts and tag friends.

2. Leverage Instagram Features

- Use Reels for higher reach and discoverability.

- Go Live to create real-time interaction with your audience.

- Utilize Instagram Shopping if applicable, linking directly to brand products.

3. Respond to Comments and Messages

Show that you're actively engaging with your followers by replying to comments, DMs, and mentions. This fosters a sense of community and increases trust, making your sponsored content more effective.

Measuring and Showcasing Your Impact

Brands want to see results from collaborations, so you need to track and present your performance effectively.

1. Track Key Metrics

Monitor:

- Engagement rate – Likes, comments, shares, and saves.

- Click-through rate (CTR) – The percentage of followers clicking on brand links.

- Conversions – Sales, sign-ups, or other measurable actions.

Use Instagram Insights or third-party tools like Later, Hootsuite, or Sprout Social to analyze performance.

2. Provide Post-Campaign Reports

A professional influencer doesn't just complete a campaign and move on. After a brand collaboration, prepare a report that includes:

- Screenshots of engagement metrics.

- A breakdown of audience reach and interactions.

- Qualitative feedback from followers.

- Recommendations for future campaigns.

This shows professionalism and increases your chances of securing long-term partnerships.

Going Beyond a Single Campaign

To create lasting relationships with brands:

- **Offer Additional Value** – Provide extra Story mentions or an exclusive IG Live session.

- **Suggest Long-Term Collaborations** – Propose multi-post deals or ambassador programs.

- **Stay in Touch** – Keep brands updated on audience growth and new content strategies.

Conclusion

Delivering value to brands goes beyond posting a sponsored photo. By creating authentic, high-quality content, engaging your audience, and showcasing your campaign results, you can establish yourself as a valuable partner. Consistently providing measurable impact will not only help you secure brand deals but also pave the way for long-term collaborations, boosting your career as an Instagram content creator.

7.3 Maximizing Instagram Live for Sales

7.3.1 Hosting Engaging Live Sessions

Introduction

Instagram Live is a powerful feature that allows users to broadcast real-time video to their followers, fostering direct interaction and engagement. Whether you are a brand, influencer, or small business, hosting an engaging live session can help you connect with your audience, promote products, and build trust. This section will cover essential strategies to create high-quality, interactive, and effective Instagram Live sessions that captivate viewers and drive engagement.

Benefits of Using Instagram Live

Before diving into the best practices, it's important to understand why Instagram Live is an essential tool for growing your presence on the platform:

- **Real-time engagement:** Allows instant interaction with your audience through comments and questions.

- **Increased visibility:** Instagram prioritizes live videos, placing them at the top of followers' feeds.

- **Authenticity:** Live sessions provide a personal and unfiltered way to communicate with your audience.

- **Promotional opportunities:** A great way to introduce new products, answer FAQs, and showcase expertise.

- **Collaboration potential:** You can co-host lives with other influencers or industry experts to expand reach.

Preparing for a Successful Live Session

1. Define Your Objectives

Before going live, determine the goal of your session. Ask yourself:

- What message do I want to convey?

- Am I educating, entertaining, or selling?

- What key takeaways should my audience have?

Having a clear objective will help structure the session and keep it focused.

2. Plan Your Content

Outline the main topics you want to cover. A rough script can help you stay on track while maintaining a natural flow. Consider structuring your session as follows:

1. **Introduction (First 2-3 minutes)**

   o Greet viewers and introduce yourself.

   o Explain the purpose of the live session.

   o Encourage engagement by asking viewers to comment or react.

2. **Main Content (10-20 minutes)**

   o Discuss your key topics in an engaging manner.

   o Share stories, examples, or demonstrations.

   o Encourage viewers to ask questions and interact.

3. **Q&A and Interaction (10 minutes)**

   o Answer audience questions in real-time.

   o Acknowledge comments to keep viewers engaged.

4. **Closing (Final 2-3 minutes)**

   o Summarize key points.

   o Provide a call to action (e.g., follow, visit website, check out a product).

   o Thank viewers for joining and encourage them to tune in next time.

3. Choose the Right Time to Go Live

Timing is crucial for maximizing viewership. Use Instagram Insights to determine when your audience is most active and schedule your live accordingly. Typically, evenings and weekends tend to have higher engagement rates.

4. Set Up a Distraction-Free Environment

Ensure your location is well-lit and quiet. Good lighting enhances video quality, and minimal background noise improves clarity. Use a tripod or phone stand to keep your camera steady.

5. Test Your Equipment and Connection

Before going live, check your internet connection and test your camera and microphone. A strong Wi-Fi connection prevents lagging and disruptions.

Engaging Your Audience During the Live Session

1. Start with Energy and Enthusiasm

First impressions matter. Begin with a warm greeting and positive energy to capture attention. Encourage viewers to participate by asking them to drop a comment or emoji.

2. Use Instagram Live Features

- **Pin Comments:** Pin an important comment (e.g., topic of discussion, CTA).
- **Use Question Stickers:** Gather questions from followers before going live.
- **Invite Guests:** Collaborate with other creators or industry experts.
- **Share Media:** Show images or videos related to your discussion.

3. Engage with Your Viewers

A successful live session is interactive. Use these strategies to maintain engagement:

- Address viewers by name when responding to comments.
- Ask open-ended questions to spark discussions.

- Encourage viewers to invite friends to join the live.

- Use polls and quizzes to keep the session fun and dynamic.

4. Maintain a Natural Flow

Avoid long pauses or awkward silences. If you experience a drop in engagement, introduce a new topic or directly address comments to re-engage viewers.

5. Monitor Analytics in Real-Time

Keep an eye on the number of viewers and engagement levels. If you notice a decline, adjust your approach by making the content more interactive or shifting topics.

Post-Live Strategies to Maximize Impact

1. Save and Share Your Live Video

After ending the session, save the video and share it on IGTV or as a Story highlight. This allows followers who missed the live to watch later.

2. Repurpose Content

Use key moments from the live session to create:

- Instagram Reels

- Carousel posts summarizing the main points

- Blog posts or YouTube videos

3. Follow Up with Your Audience

Send a thank-you message to those who engaged during the live. You can also create a post summarizing the session and encouraging further discussion in the comments.

4. Analyze Performance

Use Instagram Insights to assess:

- Number of viewers

- Engagement rate (comments, likes, shares)

- Peak viewer times

Analyzing these metrics will help improve your future live sessions.

Common Mistakes to Avoid

- **Not Promoting the Live in Advance:** Announce your live session in advance through Stories, posts, and countdown stickers.

- **Ignoring Audience Engagement:** Viewers will leave if they feel ignored. Interact consistently.

- **Poor Audio or Video Quality:** Invest in a good microphone and ensure proper lighting.

- **Rambling Without Structure:** Stay focused on your key points.

- **Ending Abruptly:** Always close with a call to action and thank viewers for their time.

Conclusion

Hosting engaging Instagram Live sessions requires preparation, interaction, and post-live strategy. By setting clear objectives, using Instagram's features effectively, and keeping your audience engaged, you can create live sessions that strengthen your brand, increase engagement, and drive conversions. Start experimenting with Instagram Live and refine your approach based on feedback and analytics for ongoing success!

7.3.2 Selling Products in Real Time

Introduction

Instagram Live has become a powerful tool for brands, influencers, and entrepreneurs to connect with their audience in real time. Beyond engagement, it offers an excellent opportunity to sell products instantly. Live selling allows businesses to showcase products, demonstrate their use, answer customer questions, and create a sense of urgency that drives purchases. In this section, we will explore how to maximize Instagram Live for real-time product sales effectively.

Understanding Instagram Live Shopping

Instagram Live Shopping enables sellers to tag products from their Instagram Shop during live broadcasts. Viewers can tap on the product link, view details, and purchase without leaving the app. This seamless integration makes live selling a lucrative method for e-commerce businesses, especially in industries such as fashion, beauty, electronics, and home goods.

Benefits of Selling on Instagram Live

1. **Real-Time Engagement:** Unlike pre-recorded videos, live sessions allow direct interaction with viewers, creating a personalized shopping experience.

2. **Increased Conversion Rates:** Customers feel more confident purchasing when they see products in action and get their questions answered immediately.

3. **Exclusive Promotions:** Offering limited-time discounts or exclusive deals during live sessions encourages impulse buying.

4. **Stronger Brand Trust:** Live selling humanizes your brand, making it more relatable and trustworthy.

5. **Enhanced Visibility:** Instagram often prioritizes live content, pushing it to the top of followers' feeds and increasing reach.

Preparing for a Successful Live Selling Session

1. Choose the Right Products

Select products that are visually appealing, easy to demonstrate, and relevant to your audience. If possible, feature bestsellers or new arrivals to create excitement.

2. Promote Your Live Session in Advance

Use Instagram Stories, feed posts, and countdown stickers to inform your audience about the upcoming live sale. Provide details such as the date, time, featured products, and any exclusive deals available during the session.

3. Ensure a Professional Setup

- **Good Lighting:** Use ring lights or natural light to ensure clear visuals.

- **Stable Camera Position:** Use a tripod or phone stand to avoid shaky footage.

- **High-Quality Audio:** Ensure clear sound, using a microphone if necessary.

- **Minimal Background Noise:** Choose a quiet location to maintain focus on your presentation.

4. Prepare an Engaging Script

While live videos should be natural and conversational, having a rough script ensures you cover key points such as:

- Introduction and greetings

- Highlighting featured products

- Demonstrating product benefits

- Encouraging engagement through Q&A

- Closing with a strong call-to-action

Engaging Your Audience During the Live Session

1. Start with an Enthusiastic Introduction

Greet your viewers warmly, introduce yourself and your brand, and briefly outline what they can expect during the live session. Create excitement by mentioning exclusive deals or giveaways.

2. Showcase and Demonstrate Products Effectively

- Hold the product close to the camera to highlight details.

- Demonstrate its use in real time.

- Share personal experiences or customer testimonials to build credibility.

- Use different angles to show the product's full appearance.

3. Encourage Real-Time Interaction

- Ask open-ended questions to keep the audience engaged.

- Respond to comments and answer questions immediately.

- Encourage viewers to use reaction emojis to express interest.

- Mention names when responding to create a personalized experience.

4. Create a Sense of Urgency

- Offer exclusive discounts available only during the live session.

- Use phrases like "Only 10 left in stock!" or "This deal ends when the live ends!"

- Set a countdown timer for special offers.

5. Leverage Co-Hosting and Influencers

Collaborate with influencers, brand ambassadors, or industry experts to expand your reach and credibility. Co-hosted sessions often attract larger audiences and boost engagement.

Closing the Live Session with a Strong Call-to-Action

As the session nears its end, summarize the key highlights and direct viewers on what to do next:

- Remind them of the special offers.

- Provide a link to your Instagram Shop or website.

- Encourage them to follow for future live sessions.

- Offer incentives such as free shipping for immediate purchases.

Post-Live Strategies for Maximizing Sales

1. Save and Share the Live Video

Instagram allows you to save your live session as an IGTV video or Story highlight. This extends the lifespan of your sales content and allows late viewers to watch and shop.

2. Engage with Viewers Who Showed Interest

- DM users who asked questions but didn't purchase.

- Offer personalized recommendations based on their inquiries.

- Send reminders about limited-time deals.

3. Analyze Performance Metrics

Use Instagram Insights to evaluate:

- Number of viewers and peak engagement times.

- Comments, likes, and shares.

- Conversion rates and sales generated from the session. Adjust future strategies based on these insights.

Conclusion

Selling products in real time on Instagram Live is a game-changer for businesses looking to increase conversions and build strong customer relationships. By preparing effectively, engaging your audience, and leveraging Instagram's shopping features, you can create an interactive and profitable shopping experience. Implement these best practices, and you'll be well on your way to mastering live selling on Instagram.

7.3.3 Answering Audience Questions Effectively

Instagram Live is a powerful tool for engaging with your audience in real time, and one of its most valuable features is the ability to interact directly with viewers through Q&A sessions. Answering audience questions effectively can boost engagement, establish your credibility, and increase sales. This section will guide you through the best practices for handling audience questions during an Instagram Live session, ensuring a smooth and productive experience.

1. Why Audience Engagement Matters in Instagram Live

Answering audience questions effectively during an Instagram Live session is crucial for several reasons:

- **Builds Trust**: Engaging with your audience in real time makes your brand or persona more authentic and relatable.

- **Encourages Interaction**: The more you interact with viewers, the more likely they are to stay and participate in future sessions.

- **Boosts Visibility**: Instagram's algorithm favors accounts with high engagement, meaning a well-handled Q&A session can increase your reach.

- **Drives Sales**: If you are selling a product or service, answering questions directly can help potential customers make purchasing decisions.

2. Preparing for a Successful Q&A Session

Announce Your Live Q&A in Advance

Let your audience know about your upcoming Instagram Live session through:

- Instagram Stories with countdown stickers

- Posts or Reels announcing the Live event

- Reminders in your captions and bio

Encouraging followers to submit questions beforehand ensures you have relevant topics to address.

Have a Clear Structure

A structured Q&A session keeps the conversation flowing and prevents awkward silences. Consider the following:

1. **Introduction** – Greet viewers, introduce the topic, and outline the session format.

2. **Main Q&A Section** – Address pre-submitted and live audience questions.

3. **Closing Remarks** – Summarize key points, encourage further engagement, and promote relevant products or services.

Prepare Pre-Submitted Questions

Before going live, collect common questions related to your topic. This ensures that even if live participation is low, you still have meaningful content to discuss.

Set Up Your Environment

- **Good Lighting**: Ensure you are well-lit and visible.

- **Clear Audio**: Use an external microphone if needed to improve sound quality.

- **Stable Internet Connection**: Avoid connectivity issues by using a strong Wi-Fi network.

- **Minimal Distractions**: Choose a quiet space with minimal background noise.

3. Managing Questions During the Live Session

Reading and Selecting Questions

Instagram Live displays viewer questions in the comments or through the dedicated Q&A feature. Here's how to handle them effectively:

- **Prioritize Relevant Questions**: Focus on those that align with your topic or sales goals.

- **Acknowledge Repetitive Questions**: If many people ask the same thing, address it collectively to save time.

- **Skip Off-Topic or Inappropriate Questions**: Maintain professionalism by ignoring or deleting irrelevant comments.

Answering Questions Clearly and Concisely

- **Repeat the Question**: This ensures clarity for viewers who may have missed it.

- **Provide a Direct Answer**: Keep responses clear and informative.

- **Give Examples**: Real-life scenarios or success stories make your answers more relatable.

Engaging with the Audience

- **Use Viewers' Names**: Personalization helps build a stronger connection.

- **Encourage More Questions**: Invite viewers to ask follow-ups for a dynamic discussion.

- **Use Polls and Emoji Reactions**: These interactive features keep engagement high.

4. Handling Challenging Questions

Answering Difficult or Technical Questions

If a question is highly technical:

- Break it down into simple terms.

- Direct viewers to additional resources (e.g., blog posts, product pages).

- Admit when you don't know something and offer to follow up later.

Addressing Negative or Critical Comments

- **Stay Professional**: Avoid defensive reactions.

- **Acknowledge Constructive Criticism**: Show that you value feedback and provide a balanced response.

- **Ignore or Block Trolls**: Don't waste time engaging with disruptive viewers.

5. Turning Q&A Sessions into Sales Opportunities

Subtly Integrate Your Products or Services

- If a question relates to your offerings, mention how they provide a solution.

- Use phrases like:

  o "That's a great question! Our [product/service] can help with that by…"

  o "Many of our customers have faced this issue, and they found that [product/service] worked really well."

Offer Limited-Time Deals

Encourage viewers to take immediate action by providing exclusive discounts during the Live session.

Redirect to Your Sales Channels

- **Call-to-Action (CTA)**: End with clear instructions, such as:
    - "If you want to learn more, visit [website link] or check out our latest post."
    - "Click the link in my bio to shop now."

6. Post-Live Follow-Up

Save and Share the Live Video

Instagram allows you to save Live sessions to IGTV or as a Story Highlight. This helps viewers who missed it catch up later.

Continue the Conversation

- Reply to comments and DMs from viewers who asked questions.
- Create follow-up content (e.g., a Q&A recap post or Reel).

Analyze Performance

Check Instagram Insights to review:

- **Viewership Duration**: How long people stayed engaged.
- **Top Questions**: Which topics gained the most interest.
- **Conversion Rates**: Did the Live session lead to sales or website visits?

7. Key Takeaways

- **Preparation is key** – Announce your Live event in advance, set a structure, and prepare common questions.
- **Engagement drives success** – Interact with your audience using clear, concise answers and personalized responses.

- **Professionalism matters** – Stay composed, handle difficult questions gracefully, and maintain a friendly tone.

- **Turn Q&A into sales** – Seamlessly introduce products/services and provide exclusive deals during the session.

- **Follow up** – Save the Live video, engage with viewers post-event, and analyze performance for improvement.

By mastering the art of answering audience questions effectively, you can build stronger relationships with your followers, enhance brand credibility, and ultimately drive business growth through Instagram Live.

Example: A Successful Instagram Live Q&A for Sales

Scenario

Emma is a small business owner who sells handmade skincare products. She decides to host an Instagram Live session to engage with her audience and answer their questions about skincare and her products. Her goal is to build trust, educate her audience, and drive sales.

Step 1: Preparation

Before going live, Emma:

- **Announces the session** a week in advance via an Instagram post and Stories with a countdown timer.

- **Asks followers to submit questions** about skincare and her products.

- **Prepares a structure**:

  1. Introduction

  2. Answering pre-submitted questions

  3. Live Q&A from the audience

  4. Exclusive discount for viewers

5. Closing remarks

Step 2: Engaging with Viewers Live

Opening the Live Session

Emma starts her Instagram Live with enthusiasm:

"Hey everyone! Welcome to my live Q&A about skincare and how to find the best products for your skin type. I'm Emma, founder of GlowNaturals, and today I'll be answering all your questions and giving you some exclusive deals at the end, so stay tuned!"

She welcomes new viewers and encourages them to ask questions using the Q&A feature.

Step 3: Answering Questions Effectively

Example 1: Handling a Common Question

💬 *Question from @skincarelover123*: "How do I know which moisturizer is best for dry skin?"

✅ **Emma's Response:**
*"Great question! If you have dry skin, look for ingredients like hyaluronic acid and shea butter—they provide deep hydration. Our **HydraGlow Moisturizer** is specifically designed for dry skin and contains both! I've seen amazing results from customers who struggled with dryness before using it."*

📌 **Pro Tip:** Emma subtly integrates her product into her response while still providing valuable, general skincare advice.

Example 2: Engaging the Audience with Personalization

💬 *Question from @jenny_beauty*: "What's the best way to use a face serum?"

✅ **Emma's Response:**
"Hey Jenny! Thanks for your question. The best way to use a serum is to apply it right after

cleansing, while your skin is still damp. This helps with absorption. For example, our Vitamin C Serum works best in the morning before applying sunscreen. What type of serum are you using now?"

📌 **Why This Works:**

- She **mentions the viewer's name** for a personal touch.

- She **provides a clear answer** with a simple skincare routine.

- She **asks a follow-up question** to keep Jenny engaged.

Example 3: Handling a Difficult Question

💬 *Question from @eco-conscious_: "Are your products cruelty-free and sustainable?"*

✅ **Emma's Response:**
"That's a fantastic question, and I really appreciate you asking about sustainability! Yes, all our products are cruelty-free, and we use eco-friendly packaging made from recycled materials. I truly believe in creating skincare that's kind to both your skin and the planet. If you'd like, I can share more about our sustainability efforts—just drop a 🌿 in the comments!"

📌 **Why This Works:**

- She **acknowledges the importance** of the question.

- She **provides a clear and confident answer**.

- She **encourages further engagement** by inviting more questions.

Step 4: Encouraging Sales Without Being Pushy

💬 *Question from @glowupgirl_: "What's the best product for glowing skin?"*

✅ **Emma's Response:**
*"If you're looking for glowing skin, exfoliation is key! Our **Glow Exfoliating Scrub** is one of our best sellers because it gently removes dead skin cells and reveals a natural glow. And for*

*everyone watching today's Live, I'm offering a 20% discount on it for the next 24 hours! Just use the code **LIVEGLOW20** at checkout."*

📌 **Why This Works:**

- She gives **a genuine skincare tip**.

- She introduces her product **naturally** into the conversation.

- She offers an **exclusive discount** for Live viewers, creating urgency.

Step 5: Closing the Live Session

Before ending, Emma:

- **Thanks her audience**: *"I loved answering your questions today! Thank you for joining and making this a fun and interactive session."*

- **Reminds viewers of the special discount**: *"Remember, the 20% discount code **LIVEGLOW20** is only available for 24 hours, so don't miss out!"*

- **Encourages further engagement**: *"If you have more questions, feel free to DM me or check out our latest post where I'll be answering more skincare tips."*

📌 **Why This Works:**

- She **reinforces the urgency** of the discount.

- She **invites post-Live engagement** to keep the conversation going.

Step 6: Post-Live Engagement

After the session, Emma:

✅ **Saves the Live video** to IGTV so followers can watch later.

✅ **Answers remaining questions** in DMs and comments.

✅ **Analyzes Instagram Insights** to check engagement and sales data.

Results & Impact

Because of her well-structured and engaging Q&A session, Emma:

✓ **Boosts engagement**—her Live reaches 3x more people than usual.

✓ **Builds trust**—viewers appreciate her transparency and knowledge.

✓ **Drives sales**—she sells 50+ units of her Glow Exfoliating Scrub within 24 hours.

Key Takeaways from Emma's Instagram Live Q&A Success

◆ **Prepare in Advance** – Promote your Live, structure your Q&A, and gather pre-submitted questions.

◆ **Answer Questions Clearly** – Be direct, provide value, and engage with the audience.

◆ **Handle Tough Questions Professionally** – Stay calm, acknowledge concerns, and give honest responses.

◆ **Subtly Promote Your Products** – Integrate products naturally into the conversation instead of forcing sales.

◆ **Follow Up After the Live** – Engage with viewers in DMs, comments, and Stories.

By following these strategies, you too can turn Instagram Live Q&A sessions into a powerful sales and engagement tool!

CHAPTER VII
Staying Safe and Managing Your Account

8.1 Privacy and Security Settings

8.1.1 Adjusting Your Privacy Controls

Introduction

Privacy is a crucial aspect of using Instagram, especially for those who want to control their digital footprint and manage their online presence effectively. Instagram offers various privacy settings that allow users to regulate who can see their content, interact with them, and access their personal information. This section provides a detailed guide on adjusting your privacy controls to ensure a safer and more comfortable experience on the platform.

1. Understanding Instagram Privacy Settings

Before adjusting your settings, it is essential to understand the different privacy features Instagram provides. These settings allow you to:

- Control who can see your posts and stories.
- Restrict who can send you direct messages (DMs) or comment on your posts.
- Manage your activity status.
- Block or report unwanted users.
- Adjust data-sharing settings with third-party apps.

By learning how these settings work, you can tailor your Instagram experience to match your personal preferences and security needs.

2. Switching Between Public and Private Accounts

Instagram allows users to choose between a **public** and **private** account:

- **Public Account**: Anyone can see your posts, stories, and followers list. Your content may appear on the Explore page and hashtag searches, making it accessible to a broad audience.

- **Private Account**: Only approved followers can see your content. Your posts and stories will not appear in public searches or Explore.

How to Set Your Account to Private:

1. Open the **Instagram app** and go to your **profile**.

2. Tap the **menu icon** (three lines) in the top right corner.

3. Select **Settings and Privacy**.

4. Tap **Account Privacy**.

5. Toggle on **Private Account**.

6. Confirm your selection.

Once your account is private, new followers must send a request for approval before they can see your posts.

3. Managing Who Can See Your Stories

Instagram Stories can be customized for different audiences. Even if your account is public, you can restrict specific people from viewing your stories.

How to Adjust Story Privacy Settings:

1. Open **Settings and Privacy**.

2. Tap **Story** under the **How Others Can Interact With You** section.

3. Choose from the following options:

- o **Hide Story From**: Select users who should not see your stories.

- o **Close Friends**: Create a list of people who can see exclusive stories.

- o **Allow Replies and Reactions**: Choose whether everyone, only followers, or no one can reply to your stories.

You can update this list anytime based on your comfort level.

4. Controlling Who Can Comment on Your Posts

Comments can significantly impact your Instagram experience, and managing them properly ensures a positive interaction space.

How to Restrict or Block Comments:

1. Go to **Settings and Privacy**.

2. Tap **Comments**.

3. Modify settings:

   - o **Allow Comments From**: Choose everyone, only people you follow, or only followers.

   - o **Block Comments From**: Add specific users to prevent them from commenting.

   - o **Filter Offensive Comments**: Enable automatic filtering of inappropriate comments.

   - o **Manual Filter**: Add specific keywords to block comments containing those words.

These options help maintain a respectful and engaging environment on your profile.

5. Managing Direct Messages (DMs)

Instagram allows you to control who can send you messages and how they appear in your inbox.

How to Adjust DM Privacy Settings:

1. Go to **Settings and Privacy**.

2. Tap **Messages and Calls**.

3. Customize options:

    o **Allow Messages From**: Decide who can send you messages (everyone, people you follow, etc.).

    o **Message Requests**: Choose whether messages from unknown users go to your message requests or are blocked.

    o **Limit Spam and Unwanted DMs**: Enable filters to prevent spam messages.

By tweaking these settings, you can avoid unwanted interactions and improve your overall experience.

6. Adjusting Activity Status and Online Presence

Instagram shows when you are online to your followers or people you chat with, but you can control this visibility.

How to Hide Your Online Status:

1. Open **Settings and Privacy**.

2. Tap **Activity Status**.

3. Toggle off **Show Activity Status**.

When disabled, others will not see when you are active, and you will also not see their activity status.

7. Restricting, Blocking, and Reporting Users

If you encounter unwanted interactions, Instagram provides several tools to limit or remove access to your profile.

Restricting a User:

- The user will not know they are restricted.

- Their comments on your posts will only be visible to them.

- Their messages will move to your request folder.

Blocking a User:

- The blocked person cannot view your profile, posts, or stories.

- They will not receive notifications about being blocked.

Reporting a User:

- Report users for harassment, spam, or inappropriate content.

- Instagram reviews reports and takes necessary actions.

How to Restrict, Block, or Report:

1. Go to the **user's profile**.

2. Tap the **three-dot menu**.

3. Choose **Restrict**, **Block**, or **Report**.

8. Managing Third-Party App Permissions

Some apps request access to your Instagram data, which may compromise privacy.

How to Review and Remove Third-Party Apps:

1. Open **Settings and Privacy**.

2. Tap **Apps and Websites**.

3. Review the connected apps and remove any that you do not trust.

Regularly checking this list helps protect your personal information from unauthorized access.

9. Keeping Your Account Secure

Beyond privacy settings, securing your account is equally important.

Essential Security Tips:

- **Use a Strong Password**: Combine letters, numbers, and symbols.

- **Enable Two-Factor Authentication (2FA)**: Adds an extra layer of protection.

- **Watch Out for Phishing Scams**: Do not click on suspicious links.

- **Regularly Update Your App**: Ensures you have the latest security features.

Conclusion

Adjusting your Instagram privacy settings allows you to create a safer and more controlled online experience. Whether it's limiting who sees your posts, restricting comments, managing DMs, or blocking unwanted users, these settings help you maintain your desired level of privacy. By following these guidelines, you can enjoy Instagram with confidence while keeping your personal information secure.

8.1.2 Protecting Your Account from Hackers

In the digital age, social media platforms like Instagram are prime targets for hackers looking to steal personal information, spread spam, or take control of accounts for malicious purposes. Protecting your Instagram account from hackers is crucial to ensure your privacy, safeguard your content, and prevent unauthorized access. This section will guide you through essential security measures to protect your account and maintain a safe social media experience.

Why Hackers Target Instagram Accounts

Before diving into security measures, it is important to understand why hackers target Instagram accounts. Some common motives include:

- **Identity Theft** – Hackers can use your personal data to impersonate you or commit fraud.

- **Scamming and Phishing** – Stolen accounts are often used to send spam or scam messages to followers.

- **Brand or Business Exploitation** – If you have a business account, hackers may use it to deceive customers or request payments fraudulently.

- **Ransom and Extortion** – Some hackers take control of accounts and demand payment in exchange for returning access.

- **Selling High-Following Accounts** – Accounts with a large follower base are valuable and can be sold illegally on the dark web.

To prevent these threats, Instagram provides several built-in security features that users should take advantage of.

Essential Steps to Secure Your Instagram Account

1. Use a Strong and Unique Password

One of the simplest but most effective ways to protect your account is by using a strong password. Here's how to create a secure password:

- Use a **mix of uppercase and lowercase letters, numbers, and special characters** (e.g., @, #, !).

- Ensure your password is **at least 12-16 characters long**.

- Avoid using personal information such as your name, birthday, or common words.

- Never reuse passwords from other accounts, especially for important services like email or banking.

- Consider using a **password manager** to generate and store secure passwords.

2. Enable Two-Factor Authentication (2FA)

Two-factor authentication adds an extra layer of security by requiring a second form of verification in addition to your password. This makes it significantly harder for hackers to access your account.

To enable 2FA on Instagram:

1. Open the Instagram app and go to **Settings**.

2. Navigate to **Security > Two-Factor Authentication**.

3. Select a preferred method:

- o **Authentication App (Recommended)** – Use apps like Google Authenticator or Authy for secure codes.

- o **Text Message (SMS)** – Receive a code via SMS (less secure than an authentication app).

- o **WhatsApp** – Available in some regions for 2FA verification.

4. Follow the on-screen instructions to complete the setup.

Tip: If you use an authentication app, **save backup codes** provided by Instagram in case you lose access to your device.

3. Keep Your Email Secure

Since Instagram account recovery relies heavily on your email, securing your email account is just as important as protecting Instagram itself.

- Use **a different, strong password** for your email.

- Enable **two-factor authentication** on your email account.

- Regularly monitor your email for any suspicious login attempts.

- Avoid clicking on suspicious links in emails that claim to be from Instagram (check the sender's email address carefully).

4. Be Cautious of Phishing Attempts

Phishing is a common method used by hackers to trick users into revealing login credentials. These scams often involve fake emails, websites, or direct messages pretending to be from Instagram.

- **Check the sender's email address** – Official Instagram emails come from "@mail.instagram.com".

- **Avoid clicking on suspicious links** – If an email asks you to log in, always go directly to Instagram's website instead.

- **Enable the "Emails from Instagram" feature** – You can check legitimate emails sent by Instagram in **Settings > Security > Emails from Instagram**.

- **Never share your password** with anyone claiming to be Instagram support. Instagram will never ask for your login details.

5. Monitor Active Logins and Devices

Instagram allows you to see where your account is logged in from. Checking this regularly can help you detect unauthorized access.

To review active logins:

1. Go to **Settings > Security > Login Activity**.

2. Check all devices and locations listed.

3. If you see an unfamiliar device or location, tap **Log Out** and change your password immediately.

6. Avoid Using Public or Shared Devices

Logging into Instagram on public computers or shared devices increases the risk of your credentials being stolen. If you must use a public computer:

- **Never save your password** on the device.

- **Use private/incognito mode** to prevent login information from being stored.

- **Log out completely** after using Instagram.

7. Be Careful with Third-Party Apps and Services

Some third-party apps claim to provide analytics, follower growth, or automation services, but many are unsafe and can compromise your account.

- **Only use official Instagram-approved apps** from trusted sources.

- **Regularly review connected apps** by going to **Settings > Security > Apps and Websites**.

- **Revoke access** to any suspicious apps that you don't recognize.

8. Update Your Instagram App and Device Regularly

Keeping your Instagram app and device software up to date helps protect against security vulnerabilities.

- Enable **automatic updates** for Instagram in your app store settings.

- Regularly update your **operating system** (iOS or Android) to receive the latest security patches.

What to Do If Your Account Gets Hacked

Despite taking precautions, hacking incidents can still happen. If you lose access to your Instagram account, follow these steps:

1. **Try Resetting Your Password**

   o   On the login page, tap **Forgot password?** and enter your email or username to receive a reset link.

2. **Check Your Email for Security Alerts**

   o   Instagram will notify you via email if your email address or password has been changed. If you receive such an email and did not authorize the change, **revert it immediately** using the link provided.

3. **Use the "Help Us Recover Your Account" Feature**

   o   On the login page, tap **Need more help?** and follow the instructions to verify your identity.

4. **Report the Hacked Account to Instagram**

   o   Go to **Instagram's Help Center** and submit a request under "Hacked Accounts."

5. **Enable Additional Security Measures Once You Regain Access**

   o   Immediately change your password and enable two-factor authentication.

   o   Review login activity and remove any unrecognized devices.

Final Thoughts

Protecting your Instagram account from hackers requires a proactive approach. By using strong passwords, enabling two-factor authentication, being aware of phishing scams, and monitoring login activity, you can significantly reduce the risk of unauthorized access.

A secure Instagram account ensures a safer social media experience, allowing you to enjoy connecting with friends, sharing content, and growing your presence without fear of hacking threats.

8.1.3 Reporting and Blocking Unwanted Users

Instagram is a social platform where people connect, share, and interact. However, as with any online space, users may encounter unwanted behavior, including spam accounts, harassment, or offensive content. Instagram provides robust features to help users report and block accounts that violate its guidelines. In this section, you'll learn how to use these features effectively to maintain a safe and enjoyable experience on the platform.

Understanding Instagram's Community Guidelines

Before reporting or blocking someone, it's essential to understand Instagram's **Community Guidelines**. Instagram prohibits:

- **Harassment and bullying** – Including hate speech, threats, or targeted attacks.

- **Spam and scams** – Fake accounts, misleading ads, and phishing attempts.

- **Violence and harmful content** – Graphic violence, self-harm encouragement, or terrorism-related content.

- **Sexually explicit content** – Nudity or sexually suggestive material (with limited exceptions for educational or artistic content).

- **Misinformation** – Spreading false information, particularly related to health or politics.

When a user violates these guidelines, you can report their account, posts, or messages to Instagram for review.

How to Report an Account, Post, or Message

Instagram offers different ways to report inappropriate behavior.

1. Reporting an Account

If someone is consistently violating Instagram's rules, you can report their entire profile.

Steps to report an account:

1. Go to the profile of the user you want to report.

2. Tap the three dots **(:) in the top-right corner** of their profile.

3. Select **"Report"** from the menu.

4. Choose **"It's inappropriate"** or **"It's spam"** based on the issue.

5. Follow the on-screen instructions to provide more details.

Instagram will review the account and may take action if it violates the guidelines.

2. Reporting a Post

If you come across a post that contains offensive, misleading, or inappropriate content, you can report it directly.

Steps to report a post:

1. Tap the **three dots (:)** in the top-right corner of the post.

2. Select **"Report"** from the options.

3. Choose a reason for reporting (e.g., hate speech, violence, false information).

4. Submit your report.

Instagram reviews flagged posts and may remove them if they break the rules.

3. Reporting a Comment

Hurtful or offensive comments can be reported individually.

Steps to report a comment:

1. Swipe left on the comment (on iOS) or press and hold the comment (on Android).

2. Tap the **exclamation mark (!) or "Report"** option.

3. Choose why you are reporting the comment (e.g., hate speech, harassment).

4. Submit your report.

If a comment is violating Instagram's policies, it may be removed, and the user may be warned or penalized.

4. Reporting a Direct Message (DM)

If someone sends you offensive or spam messages, you can report the conversation.

Steps to report a DM:

1. Open the chat in Instagram Direct Messages.

2. Tap and hold the specific message you want to report.

3. Select **"Report"** and choose the reason for reporting.

4. Confirm your report submission.

Instagram may restrict or remove accounts that send repeated offensive messages.

Blocking Unwanted Users

Sometimes, reporting alone is not enough. If a user is bothering you personally, blocking them is the best solution. When you block someone, they can no longer:

- View your posts, stories, or profile.

- Send you messages or comments.

- Tag you in posts or stories.

How to Block a User

1. Visit the profile of the person you want to block.

2. Tap the **three dots (⋮)** in the top-right corner.

3. Select **"Block"** from the menu.

4. Confirm your choice.

Blocked users are not notified, but they will no longer be able to interact with you.

Blocking vs. Restricting: What's the Difference?

- **Blocking** completely prevents the person from interacting with you.

- **Restricting** limits their interactions without notifying them (e.g., their comments won't be visible to others, and they won't see when you're online).

How to Restrict a User:

1. Go to the user's profile.

2. Tap the **three dots (⋮)** and select **"Restrict"**.

3. Confirm your choice.

This feature is helpful for dealing with minor nuisances without escalating the situation.

Managing Your Blocked List

If you ever change your mind, you can manage your blocked accounts.

How to Unblock Someone:

1. Go to **Settings > Privacy**.

2. Scroll down to **Blocked Accounts**.

3. Tap on the user you want to unblock.

4. Select **"Unblock"** and confirm.

Unblocked users will be able to see your content again, but they won't be automatically refollowed.

Additional Safety Measures

To enhance your security, consider enabling the following features:

1. Filtering Offensive Content Automatically

Instagram allows you to filter offensive words and phrases from comments and messages.

Steps to enable content filtering:

1. Go to Settings > Privacy > Hidden Words.

2. Toggle on "Hide Offensive Comments" and "Hide More Comments".

3. You can also add custom words to filter specific terms.

2. Turning Off Message Requests

If you receive too many unwanted messages, you can prevent strangers from messaging you.

Steps to disable message requests:

1. Go to Settings > Privacy > Messages.

2. Under Other People, select "Don't Receive Requests".

3. Enabling Comment Restrictions

If you don't want comments from strangers, you can limit them.

Steps to restrict comments:

1. Go to Settings > Privacy > Comments.

2. Under Comment Controls, choose who can comment (e.g., only people you follow).

What Happens After Reporting?

Once you report a user, Instagram will review the case. If they find a violation, they may:

- Remove the content.

- Warn or temporarily suspend the user.

- Permanently ban repeat offenders.

However, not all reports result in immediate action. If Instagram doesn't remove the content, but you still feel unsafe, blocking the user is the best step.

Final Thoughts

Instagram is a powerful platform, but it's essential to maintain control over your experience. Knowing how to **report, block, and restrict unwanted users** ensures a safe, positive, and enjoyable time on the app. By taking advantage of Instagram's privacy and security settings, you can protect yourself from harassment, spam, and other unwanted interactions.

If you ever feel unsafe, don't hesitate to use these tools and report problematic behavior. Your well-being and safety always come first!

8.2 Dealing with Negative Comments and Trolls

8.2.1 Moderating Your Comments Section

Introduction

Instagram is a platform built for engagement, and the comments section is where much of that interaction happens. Whether you are a casual user, influencer, or business, managing your comments effectively is crucial for maintaining a positive and professional online presence. While constructive discussions and positive interactions can foster a strong community, negative comments and spam can harm your reputation and deter genuine followers.

This section will guide you through best practices for moderating your comments, tools available within Instagram to help with moderation, and strategies to maintain a healthy and engaging community.

Understanding the Importance of Comment Moderation

1. Building a Positive Community

A well-moderated comments section encourages respectful conversations, making your page a welcoming space for followers. If your comments are filled with negativity, spam, or inappropriate content, it can drive away genuine engagement and diminish the quality of your audience interactions.

2. Protecting Your Brand Image

For businesses and influencers, the comments section is often the first place potential followers and customers check when evaluating credibility. Negative, offensive, or misleading comments can damage your brand image and reduce trust in your content or services.

3. Encouraging Healthy Engagement

By moderating comments, you can ensure that discussions remain productive and meaningful. This, in turn, fosters more engagement and encourages users to interact with your content positively.

Instagram's Built-In Comment Moderation Tools

1. Filter and Restrict Comments Automatically

Instagram offers several features that allow users to automatically filter out harmful or inappropriate comments:

- **Manual Keyword Filtering**: You can set up a list of keywords that Instagram will automatically block from appearing in your comments. This is useful for filtering out offensive language or spam.

- **Hidden Offensive Comments**: Instagram automatically hides comments it detects as offensive based on AI-powered moderation.

- **Restricting Users**: If a user repeatedly leaves inappropriate comments, you can restrict them, which means their comments will only be visible to them unless you approve them.

How to Enable Comment Filtering:

1. Go to your Instagram profile.

2. Tap the three-line menu in the top right corner and select **Settings**.

3. Navigate to **Privacy** > **Comments**.

4. Turn on **Hide Offensive Comments** and **Manual Filter**.

5. Add any specific words or phrases you want to filter out.

2. Turning Off Comments on Specific Posts

If you anticipate a post attracting unnecessary negativity, you can disable comments entirely. This can be useful for controversial posts or content where you want to limit discussions.

How to Disable Comments:

1. Go to the post you want to moderate.

2. Tap the three-dot menu at the top right of the post.

3. Select **Turn Off Commenting**.

3. Pinning Positive Comments

Instagram allows you to **pin comments**, highlighting them at the top of the comment section. This feature is useful for promoting constructive discussions and ensuring that the first comments new visitors see are positive.

How to Pin a Comment:

1. Swipe left on the comment you want to pin.

2. Tap the **Pin** icon.

3. The pinned comment will now appear at the top.

4. Blocking and Reporting Users

For persistent trolls or spam accounts, blocking is often the best solution. Additionally, reporting abusive or harmful comments helps Instagram improve its moderation system.

How to Block or Report a User:

1. Tap on the comment from the offending user.

2. Select **Block** or **Report**.

3. Follow the prompts to complete the action.

Best Practices for Comment Moderation

1. Establish Community Guidelines

If you are managing a large account or brand, clearly defining community guidelines helps set expectations for acceptable behavior. These can include:

- No hate speech, bullying, or harassment.

- No spamming or self-promotion.

- Respectful disagreements are encouraged, but personal attacks are not tolerated.

2. Respond to Constructive Criticism Professionally

Negative feedback isn't always trolling—sometimes, it's valuable criticism. Instead of deleting all negative comments, assess whether they offer constructive feedback and respond professionally.

Example Response to a Complaint:

- *User*: "I didn't like the quality of your product. It wasn't worth the price."

- *Response*: "We're sorry to hear that! We strive to provide the best quality. Could you send us a DM so we can resolve this issue?"

3. Use Third-Party Moderation Tools

For accounts with high engagement, Instagram's built-in tools may not be enough. Consider using third-party social media management tools like:

- Hootsuite

- Sprout Social

- Later

These tools allow you to monitor comments efficiently, assign responses to team members, and automate filtering processes.

4. Schedule Time for Comment Moderation

Consistency is key. Set aside time daily to review and moderate comments, ensuring that your engagement remains positive and constructive.

5. Engage with Your Audience

Ignoring comments—even positive ones—can make followers feel unheard. Engage actively by:

- Responding to positive comments with appreciation.

- Asking follow-up questions to spark discussions.

- Showing personality in your replies to humanize your brand.

Handling Difficult Situations

1. Dealing with Persistent Trolls

Trolls aim to provoke emotional reactions. The best strategies are:

- Ignore and restrict them.
- Avoid arguing publicly.
- Use humor when appropriate to defuse the situation.

2. Addressing Misinformation

If a user spreads false information in your comments:

- Politely correct the misinformation with factual details.
- If it's damaging, consider deleting or reporting the comment.

3. Managing Harassment and Bullying

If you or your followers experience harassment:

- Block and report the offender.
- Encourage your community to report abusive behavior.
- Consider turning off comments on sensitive posts.

Conclusion

Moderating your Instagram comments section is vital to maintaining a healthy, positive, and engaging community. By leveraging Instagram's built-in tools, setting clear guidelines, and responding to feedback professionally, you can create a welcoming space that encourages meaningful interactions.

Effective comment moderation is not about silencing criticism but about fostering constructive discussions while keeping negativity and spam in check. With the right strategies in place, your Instagram presence will remain professional, engaging, and enjoyable for both you and your audience.

Would you like to explore more advanced moderation strategies? Let's continue optimizing your Instagram experience!

8.2.2 How to Respond to Criticism

Understanding Criticism on Instagram

Criticism is an inevitable part of having a public presence on social media, including Instagram. Whether you are a personal user, a content creator, or a business, at some point, you will face feedback that may be harsh, unwarranted, or constructive. Understanding the nature of criticism is the first step to responding effectively.

Criticism generally falls into three categories:

1. **Constructive Criticism** – Feedback that is meant to help improve your content or actions.

2. **Negative but Fair Criticism** – Harsh but truthful comments about your content or actions.

3. **Unwarranted Hate or Trolling** – Comments designed to provoke a reaction rather than offer any real feedback.

Your response should be tailored to the type of criticism you receive.

Strategies for Responding to Criticism

1. Assess Before You React

Before responding to a negative comment, take a moment to analyze the intent behind it. Ask yourself:

- Is this comment constructive or destructive?

- Does this person have a valid point?

- Is it worth responding to, or should it be ignored?

- Would responding escalate the situation?

If the comment is a baseless insult or an attempt to provoke, the best response might be no response at all.

2. Acknowledge and Appreciate Constructive Criticism

If someone offers constructive criticism, acknowledge their input and show appreciation. Even if you disagree, responding politely fosters a positive image and encourages engagement.

Example responses:

- *"Thank you for your feedback! I appreciate your perspective and will take it into consideration."*

- *"I see what you mean. I'll keep that in mind for future posts. Thanks for your input!"*

- *"I understand your concerns. Let's have a discussion about how I can improve."*

This approach makes your followers feel heard and can turn a critic into a loyal supporter.

3. Stay Calm and Professional When Handling Negative Criticism

Receiving negative feedback can be frustrating, but responding with anger or defensiveness can harm your reputation. Always maintain professionalism.

Example responses:

- *"I understand that you feel this way. I appreciate you sharing your thoughts."*

- *"I respect your opinion and will take it into account."*

- *"Sorry to hear you feel that way. I strive to improve and value all feedback."*

By responding calmly, you defuse the situation and show emotional intelligence.

4. Clarify Misunderstandings

Sometimes, negative comments stem from misunderstandings. If someone criticizes you based on incorrect information, politely clarify your stance.

Example responses:

- *"I see where you're coming from, but actually, what I meant was..."*

- *"I appreciate your feedback! Just to clarify, the purpose of this post was..."*

Providing context can resolve miscommunications and prevent further negativity.

5. Know When to Ignore or Block

Some comments are not worth engaging with. If a user is repeatedly leaving hateful messages or engaging in harassment, it is best to ignore, mute, or block them.

Situations when ignoring or blocking is appropriate:

- When a user is using abusive or offensive language.

- When a user is spamming your posts with negativity.

- When engaging with them will only escalate the situation.

Instagram provides tools to restrict users, hide comments, and report harassment. Use these features when necessary.

6. Take the Conversation to Private Messages

If criticism involves a deeper issue or misunderstanding, it may be best to address it privately.

Example response:

- *"I'd love to discuss this further. Feel free to DM me so we can chat more."*

Taking the conversation off the public forum helps resolve conflicts more effectively.

Managing Your Emotions While Dealing with Criticism

Handling criticism can be emotionally draining. Here are a few tips to manage your emotions:

- **Take a break before responding.** Give yourself time to cool down.

- **Remember that criticism is not always personal.** Often, people critique content, not the creator.

- **Seek support from friends or colleagues.** Discussing negative feedback with trusted individuals can provide perspective.

- **Focus on the positive.** For every negative comment, there are likely many more positive ones.

Learning from Criticism

Not all criticism is bad. In fact, constructive criticism can help you grow. Regularly review feedback and ask yourself:

- What patterns do I see in the criticism I receive?

- Are there valid points I can use to improve my content?

- How can I handle criticism more effectively in the future?

By approaching criticism with an open mind, you turn it into a tool for personal and professional development.

Conclusion

Criticism on Instagram is inevitable, but how you respond to it defines your brand and credibility. By assessing the intent behind comments, responding professionally, and knowing when to ignore or engage, you can maintain a positive online presence. Embrace feedback as a means of growth, and always handle criticism with grace and maturity.

8.2.3 When to Ignore or Block Users

Understanding Negative Comments and Trolls

In the digital world, Instagram is a powerful tool for connecting with others, sharing content, and building a community. However, as your presence on Instagram grows, you may encounter negative comments, trolls, and even online harassment. Knowing when to engage, ignore, or block someone is essential for maintaining a positive experience on the platform.

Negative interactions on Instagram can range from constructive criticism to outright trolling. It is crucial to distinguish between feedback that can be useful and comments meant to provoke or harm. While some negativity can be addressed with engagement and professionalism, others require complete disengagement or blocking.

Identifying Harmful Interactions

Before deciding to ignore or block a user, assess the nature of their comments. Here are some common types of negative interactions:

1. **Constructive Criticism** – These comments may seem negative but are actually intended to provide valuable feedback. It is best to engage with these thoughtfully.

2. **Mild Disagreements** – Differences in opinion are normal. Responding respectfully can foster discussion rather than conflict.

3. **Spam and Scams** – Comments that promote unrelated products, services, or contain phishing links should be ignored or reported.

4. **Trolling and Harassment** – These comments are designed to provoke, offend, or harm. Trolls thrive on attention, so engagement often fuels their behavior.

5. **Hate Speech and Cyberbullying** – Any content that includes threats, racism, sexism, or other discriminatory remarks should be reported and blocked immediately.

When to Ignore Negative Comments

Ignoring negativity can be a powerful tool, especially when dealing with trolls and users who seek attention. Here are instances when ignoring a comment is the best approach:

- **The Comment is Clearly a Troll's Bait** – Trolls post inflammatory remarks to get a reaction. If you ignore them, they often lose interest and move on.

- **The Comment is Not Harmful but Unnecessary** – Some users post rude or passive-aggressive remarks that do not contribute meaningfully to the conversation. Engaging with them can escalate the situation unnecessarily.

- **The User Repeatedly Seeks Attention** – Some users comment repeatedly to provoke reactions. If their comments are not outright harmful, ignoring them can prevent further escalation.

- **You Have a Large Following and Cannot Address Everything** – If your account has a significant audience, responding to every comment is impractical. It is okay to let some negativity slide.

Strategies for Ignoring Negative Comments

- **Do Not React Emotionally** – Trolls seek emotional reactions. Staying composed ensures they do not get the satisfaction of knowing they upset you.

- **Encourage Positive Engagement** – Instead of focusing on negative comments, prioritize responding to positive and supportive messages.

- **Use Instagram's Hidden Replies Feature** – If a comment is annoying but not harmful, you can hide it without blocking the user. This prevents them from knowing they have been ignored.

When to Block Users

Blocking is a more definitive action and should be used when a user crosses a line. Here are instances when blocking is the best course of action:

- **The User is Harassing or Stalking You** – If someone continuously sends unwanted messages, leaves disturbing comments, or follows you aggressively, blocking is necessary.

- **The User is Engaging in Hate Speech or Threats** – If a comment includes discrimination, threats, or violence, blocking and reporting should be immediate actions.

- **The User is Spamming Your Posts** – If an account repeatedly posts promotional links, scams, or off-topic comments, blocking prevents further nuisance.

- **The User Continually Harasses Others in Your Comments** – If someone is targeting your followers or creating a toxic environment, blocking helps maintain a safe space for your community.

- **The User Has Been Warned But Continues the Behavior** – If you have engaged respectfully and asked the user to stop, yet they persist in being negative or abusive, blocking is the next step.

How to Block a User on Instagram

Blocking a user on Instagram is simple and ensures they can no longer see your profile, posts, or interact with you in any way. Follow these steps:

1. Navigate to the user's profile.

2. Tap the three-dot menu in the top-right corner.

3. Select **Block**.

4. Confirm your action. You can also choose to block any future accounts the person creates.

Once blocked, the user will not be notified, but they will no longer be able to interact with your content or find your profile.

Alternative Actions to Blocking

If you are hesitant to block someone completely, Instagram offers additional tools:

- **Restricting a User** – This limits what the user can do without notifying them. Their comments on your posts will only be visible to them unless you approve them.

- **Muting a User** – If a user's posts or stories are bothering you but are not harmful, you can mute them instead of blocking.

- **Reporting a User** – If a user violates Instagram's community guidelines, report them for review by Instagram.

Conclusion

Knowing when to ignore or block users is crucial for a positive Instagram experience. While some negativity can be brushed off, harmful behavior should be addressed promptly. By using Instagram's built-in tools and fostering a positive online presence, you can ensure that your interactions remain healthy and constructive. Prioritizing your mental well-being and maintaining a safe community should always come first.

8.3 Managing Multiple Accounts

8.3.1 Switching Between Personal and Business Profiles

Introduction

Instagram offers different account types to cater to various users' needs. Whether you're an individual looking to share personal moments, a content creator aiming to build a following, or a business promoting products and services, Instagram provides flexibility through **Personal, Creator, and Business accounts**. Understanding how to switch between these accounts is essential for maximizing Instagram's features and ensuring an optimized experience tailored to your goals.

This section will explore the differences between personal and business profiles, the benefits of each, step-by-step instructions on switching accounts, and best practices to manage them efficiently.

1. Understanding Instagram Account Types

Before switching between personal and business profiles, it's crucial to understand the key differences between these account types.

Personal Account

A **personal Instagram account** is the default option when signing up. It is best suited for individuals who use Instagram to connect with friends and family, share personal photos, and explore content without analytics or promotional tools.

Features of a Personal Account:

- Access to standard Instagram features (posting, stories, reels, IG Live, and direct messaging).

- Ability to set the account as private, limiting content visibility to approved followers.

- No access to **Instagram Insights** (analytics tools to track engagement and audience behavior).

- No access to **Instagram Shopping** or promotional tools.

Business Account

A **business Instagram account** is designed for brands, entrepreneurs, and organizations looking to expand their reach, promote products, and engage with customers more effectively.

Features of a Business Account:

- **Instagram Insights** to track engagement, reach, and audience demographics.

- Access to **Instagram Ads** for targeted advertising.

- Ability to create a **Shop** to sell products directly on Instagram.

- Additional contact options, such as **email, phone, and address links** in the bio.

- Access to **Auto-publishing tools** for scheduled posts.

- The account is always **public** (cannot be set to private).

Choosing the Right Account Type for Your Needs

- If you are a **casual user** who shares personal content, a **personal account** is the best fit.

- If you are a **content creator or influencer**, consider switching to a **Creator account** (a hybrid between personal and business accounts).

- If you are a **business owner**, freelancer, or marketer, a **business account** is ideal for accessing Instagram's advanced marketing tools.

2. How to Switch Between Personal and Business Profiles

Switching between Instagram accounts is a simple process that can be completed within a few steps. Follow these instructions to switch between personal and business accounts:

Switching from a Personal Account to a Business Account

1. **Open Instagram** and navigate to your profile.

2. Tap the **menu icon (☰)** in the top right corner.

3. Select **Settings and privacy**.

4. Scroll down and tap **Account type and tools**.

5. Tap **Switch to professional account**.

6. Select **Business** as your account type.

7. Follow the prompts to add details, such as **category, contact information, and business details**.

8. Connect your account to a **Facebook Page** (optional but recommended for ad management).

9. Tap **Done**, and your account will switch to a **Business profile**.

Switching from a Business Account to a Personal Account

1. **Open Instagram** and go to your profile.

2. Tap the **menu icon (☰)** and select **Settings and privacy**.

3. Tap **Account type and tools**.

4. Tap **Switch to personal account**.

5. Confirm your selection, and Instagram will revert your account to a **personal profile**.

💡 *Note:* When switching from a business account back to a personal account, you will lose access to **Instagram Insights, ad tools, and shopping features**.

Managing Multiple Accounts Efficiently

Instagram allows users to **add and manage multiple accounts** without constantly logging in and out. Follow these steps to add multiple accounts:

1. **Go to your profile** and tap the **menu icon (☰)**.

2. Tap **Settings and privacy** and scroll down to **Add account**.

3. Select **Log into existing account** or **Create new account**.

4. Once added, you can switch between accounts by **holding down your profile picture** in the bottom right corner or navigating to your profile and tapping your username.

---

3. Best Practices for Managing Personal and Business Accounts

Once you've successfully switched between personal and business accounts, here are some best practices for managing them effectively:

Keep Personal and Business Content Separate

- Maintain a **clear distinction** between personal and professional posts.
- Avoid mixing business promotions with casual personal content to maintain brand credibility.

Utilize Instagram's Scheduling and Insights

- Business accounts should take advantage of **Instagram Insights** to track engagement and audience behavior.
- Use scheduling tools like **Meta Business Suite** or third-party apps (Later, Hootsuite) to plan content in advance.

Be Consistent with Branding

- If you're switching between accounts regularly, ensure your **business profile has a professional aesthetic**, including a high-quality profile picture, branded highlights, and consistent content themes.

Protect Both Accounts

- Enable **two-factor authentication (2FA)** on both personal and business accounts for added security.
- Monitor account activity and review **login sessions** regularly to prevent unauthorized access.

Delegate Account Management if Needed

- If you're running a business, consider **adding team members** to help manage the account instead of constantly switching between accounts.

- Use Instagram's **collaborator features** to grant access without sharing login credentials.

Conclusion

Switching between personal and business profiles on Instagram is a **straightforward process**, but choosing the right account type depends on your goals. A personal account is ideal for everyday users, while a business account offers powerful tools for brand growth, analytics, and advertising.

By following best practices and efficiently managing multiple accounts, you can seamlessly transition between personal and professional content while **leveraging Instagram's features to their full potential**.

Now that you understand how to switch between account types, the next step is mastering advanced Instagram strategies to grow and monetize your presence!

8.3.2 Using Third-Party Tools for Management

Managing multiple Instagram accounts can be overwhelming, especially for businesses, influencers, and social media managers handling various brands. Fortunately, several third-party tools can streamline the process, making it easier to schedule posts, track analytics, engage with followers, and maintain consistency across different accounts. In this section, we will explore why third-party tools are beneficial, what key features to look for, and some of the best tools available for managing multiple Instagram accounts efficiently.

Why Use Third-Party Tools for Instagram Management?

1. Centralized Management

One of the main advantages of third-party tools is the ability to manage multiple Instagram accounts from a single dashboard. Instead of logging in and out of different accounts manually, these tools provide an integrated platform where users can switch between accounts seamlessly.

2. Efficient Scheduling and Automation

Scheduling tools allow users to plan and automate posts in advance. This helps maintain a consistent posting schedule, which is crucial for engagement and growth. Many platforms offer features such as automatic posting, content calendars, and reminders.

3. Advanced Analytics and Insights

While Instagram provides built-in analytics for business and creator accounts, third-party tools often offer deeper insights. Users can track follower growth, engagement rates, best posting times, and performance comparisons across different accounts.

4. Improved Engagement and Interaction

Engaging with followers across multiple accounts can be time-consuming. Third-party tools offer features like comment moderation, direct messaging, and engagement tracking, ensuring that no interaction is missed.

5. Team Collaboration

For businesses and agencies, third-party tools allow multiple team members to access and manage accounts with specific roles and permissions. This ensures efficient workflow and security.

Key Features to Look for in Third-Party Instagram Management Tools

When selecting a third-party tool, consider the following essential features:

1. Multi-Account Support

Ensure the platform supports multiple Instagram accounts and allows easy switching between them.

2. Post Scheduling and Automation

A robust scheduler should offer features like auto-posting, a visual content calendar, and post previews.

3. Analytics and Performance Tracking

Look for detailed insights into follower demographics, engagement trends, and content performance.

4. Engagement and Inbox Management

A tool should allow for replying to comments, managing direct messages, and monitoring brand mentions in a single dashboard.

5. Content Curation and Media Library

Having a repository for frequently used images, videos, and templates can save time and enhance content quality.

6. Collaboration and User Roles

For teams, the ability to assign roles (admin, editor, viewer) ensures security and efficiency.

7. Integration with Other Platforms

Some tools integrate with other social media platforms (Facebook, Twitter, LinkedIn), email marketing services, and project management tools.

Best Third-Party Tools for Managing Multiple Instagram Accounts

1. Hootsuite

- Supports multiple Instagram accounts and other social media platforms
- Provides scheduling, analytics, and team collaboration features
- Allows bulk scheduling and content planning

2. Buffer

- Simple and user-friendly scheduling tool
- Offers analytics to track performance
- Allows multiple team members to manage accounts

3. Later

- Specializes in Instagram post scheduling
- Provides a visual content calendar
- Supports automatic posting for images and videos

4. Sprout Social

- Advanced analytics and reporting features
- Centralized inbox for managing DMs and comments
- Strong collaboration tools for teams

5. Agorapulse

- Social inbox for tracking comments and messages
- Detailed reporting and competitor analysis
- Supports content queuing and scheduling

6. SocialBee

- Focuses on content recycling and automation
- Provides category-based scheduling
- Integrates with various social networks

7. Tailwind

- Designed for visual platforms like Instagram and Pinterest
- Smart scheduling and hashtag suggestions
- Drag-and-drop calendar for easy planning

How to Use Third-Party Tools Effectively

1. Set Up Your Accounts Properly

Before using any tool, connect your Instagram accounts properly by granting necessary permissions. If using a business or creator account, ensure API access is enabled.

2. Create a Posting Strategy

Use scheduling features to maintain a consistent posting schedule. Plan content weeks in advance to ensure variety and relevance.

3. Monitor Analytics Regularly

Leverage analytics to identify what type of content performs best, the best times to post, and how to optimize engagement.

4. Engage With Your Audience

Don't rely solely on automation. Take time to interact with followers by responding to comments and DMs to build genuine relationships.

5. Test and Optimize

Regularly evaluate your strategy by testing different types of content, captions, hashtags, and posting schedules. Use insights from third-party tools to refine your approach.

6. Maintain Security and Compliance

Ensure that the tool you choose complies with Instagram's terms of service. Avoid automation tools that engage in spam-like behavior, as this can lead to account suspension.

Final Thoughts

Using third-party tools for Instagram management can significantly enhance efficiency and effectiveness, especially when handling multiple accounts. By choosing the right tool based on your needs, you can streamline content scheduling, optimize engagement, analyze performance, and ensure seamless account management. However, while automation can save time, maintaining a personal touch with your audience is crucial for long-term growth. Experiment with different tools, track their effectiveness, and continuously refine your Instagram strategy for the best results.

8.3.3 Delegating Account Management

As your Instagram presence grows, managing your account effectively becomes more demanding. Whether you are an influencer, a business, or a brand, you may reach a point where you need assistance in handling daily operations, content posting, engagement, or analytics. Delegating account management can help you maintain consistency, improve efficiency, and allow you to focus on strategic decisions rather than day-to-day tasks.

1. Understanding the Need for Delegation

Before handing over control of your Instagram account to someone else, it's crucial to determine why and what aspects of management need delegation. Common reasons for delegating account management include:

- **Time Management:** Running an Instagram account, especially a business or influencer account, requires significant time for content creation, engagement, and strategy development.

- **Consistency in Posting:** Having a dedicated person ensures that content is posted regularly, even when you're unavailable.

- **Professional Content Creation:** A social media manager or content creator can enhance the quality of posts, videos, and overall branding.

- **Community Engagement:** Responding to comments, messages, and engaging with followers is time-consuming but necessary for growth.

- **Analytics and Strategy:** Delegating data analysis and strategy planning can help improve your Instagram performance.

2. Who Can Manage Your Instagram Account?

Depending on your needs and budget, you can delegate Instagram account management to various individuals or teams:

- **Social Media Managers:** Professionals who handle content creation, posting schedules, and engagement strategies.

- **Virtual Assistants:** Freelancers who can assist with scheduling posts, responding to DMs, and basic engagement tasks.

- **Marketing Agencies:** Full-service firms that manage Instagram alongside other social media platforms, often providing analytics and paid advertising strategies.

- **Team Members or Employees:** If you run a business, you may assign Instagram duties to an internal marketing team member.

- **Community Managers:** Professionals who focus on engagement, responding to comments, and fostering a strong online presence.

3. Granting Access Safely

To delegate account management securely, Instagram offers several methods to grant access without compromising security:

a. Using Instagram's Professional Dashboard

Instagram allows business and creator accounts to assign account roles through Facebook's Meta Business Suite. This method ensures controlled access and prevents unauthorized logins.

Steps to grant access via Meta Business Suite:

1. Go to business.facebook.com and log in.

2. Select the business account linked to your Instagram.

3. Navigate to "Settings" and click on "Business Settings."

4. Under "Accounts," select "Instagram Accounts."

5. Click "Add People" and assign roles such as Admin, Editor, or Moderator.

6. Save changes and ensure the person accepts the invite.

b. Sharing Login Credentials Securely

If you prefer to grant direct access, follow best security practices:

- Use a password manager like LastPass or 1Password to share credentials securely.

- Enable two-factor authentication (2FA) and require the manager to verify their login.

- Regularly update passwords and remove access if an employee or contractor leaves.

c. Using Third-Party Management Tools

Several social media management tools allow you to grant access without sharing passwords, including:

- **Hootsuite**

- **Later**

- **Buffer**

- **Sprout Social**

- **Agorapulse** These tools enable scheduling, analytics, and team collaboration without direct account logins.

4. Defining Roles and Responsibilities

Clearly defining roles ensures smooth workflow and avoids confusion. Common tasks delegated include:

- **Content Creation:** Designing graphics, taking photos, and editing videos.

- **Caption Writing & Hashtag Research:** Crafting engaging captions and selecting relevant hashtags.

- **Scheduling & Posting:** Planning a content calendar and ensuring timely uploads.

- **Engagement Management:** Replying to comments, responding to DMs, and interacting with followers.

- **Performance Analysis:** Monitoring engagement metrics, tracking growth, and suggesting strategy changes.

- **Paid Advertising:** Running and optimizing Instagram ad campaigns.

Setting clear expectations and goals helps the delegated manager understand their duties and measure success.

5. Monitoring and Evaluating Performance

Even after delegation, regularly reviewing your account's performance is essential. Some key practices include:

- **Weekly Reports:** Ask for performance reports detailing engagement, follower growth, and content insights.

- **Regular Check-ins:** Schedule bi-weekly or monthly meetings to discuss strategy adjustments.

- **Tracking Security Logs:** Check Instagram's login activity to ensure there are no unauthorized access attempts.

- **Analyzing Content Performance:** Use Instagram Insights to review which posts perform best and refine the content strategy accordingly.

6. Maintaining Security and Control

Delegation doesn't mean losing control over your Instagram account. Follow these security practices:

- **Limit Admin Access:** Only give full control to trusted individuals; others should have limited permissions.

- **Enable Two-Factor Authentication:** Adds an extra layer of security against unauthorized logins.

- **Revoke Access When Necessary:** If a manager leaves or an agency contract ends, immediately remove their access.

- **Backup Important Data:** Save copies of content, captions, and analytics reports to avoid data loss.

7. Best Practices for a Successful Delegation

- **Start Small:** Begin by delegating minor tasks and gradually increase responsibility as trust builds.

- **Use Collaboration Tools:** Slack, Trello, or Asana can improve workflow efficiency.

- **Establish Communication Protocols:** Set up guidelines for approvals, feedback, and reporting structures.

- **Encourage Creative Freedom:** Allow managers some flexibility to innovate while maintaining brand consistency.

- **Keep a Contingency Plan:** In case of mismanagement, have a plan to regain full control quickly.

Final Thoughts

Delegating Instagram account management can be a game-changer for businesses and influencers, freeing up time and enhancing engagement. However, it requires careful planning, secure access management, and ongoing supervision to ensure success. By following these best practices, you can build an effective, secure, and productive Instagram management system while maintaining control over your brand identity.

Conclusion

9.1 Recap of Key Takeaways

As we reach the end of this comprehensive guide, let's take a moment to review the key insights and lessons covered throughout the book. Whether you're a beginner just getting started on Instagram or an experienced user looking to refine your strategies, this guide has provided you with valuable knowledge to help you master the platform.

Understanding Instagram and Its Potential

Instagram is more than just a photo-sharing app; it's a powerful social media platform that allows individuals, businesses, and influencers to connect with a global audience. We explored its evolution, importance in modern digital marketing, and the various account types available—Personal, Creator, and Business—each with its own advantages.

Getting Started: Setting Up and Navigating Instagram

The foundation of success on Instagram starts with properly setting up your account. From creating a profile and choosing the right username to optimizing your bio and profile picture, the first impressions matter. We also examined the essential elements of Instagram's interface, including the Home Feed, Stories, Reels, Explore Page, and Direct Messages.

Content Creation: Posting and Engaging Effectively

Instagram is a visual-first platform, so mastering content creation is crucial. We covered the different types of content you can share, such as static posts, carousels, Stories, and Reels. Key takeaways include:

- **Creating High-Quality Posts**: Using high-resolution images, writing compelling captions, and incorporating relevant hashtags.

- **Instagram Stories**: Adding interactive elements like polls, Q&A, stickers, and highlights to boost engagement.

- **Instagram Reels**: Utilizing short-form videos to reach new audiences and enhance visibility.

- **Best Practices for Engagement**: Liking, commenting, sharing, and using Direct Messages effectively to build relationships with followers.

Building and Growing Your Audience

Growth on Instagram requires a combination of strategy, consistency, and engagement. Important lessons from this section include:

- **Understanding the Instagram Algorithm**: Factors such as engagement, relevancy, and consistency determine how content is shown to users.

- **Hashtags and Geotags**: Leveraging trending and niche hashtags to improve discoverability.

- **Collaborations and Influencer Partnerships**: Engaging with influencers and participating in community discussions to expand reach.

- **Best Posting Practices**: Finding the best times to post, creating a content calendar, and scheduling posts in advance.

Advanced Instagram Strategies

For those looking to take their Instagram presence to the next level, we explored advanced strategies including:

- **Using Instagram for Business and Branding**: Setting up an Instagram Business account, using Instagram Shopping, and creating a strong brand identity.

- **Instagram Ads and Promotions**: Running paid advertising campaigns and analyzing ad performance to maximize ROI.

- **Collaborations and Sponsored Content**: Partnering with brands and influencers to monetize content and build credibility.

Tracking Performance and Optimization

To grow successfully, tracking progress and refining strategies is essential. Key takeaways include:

- **Using Instagram Insights**: Understanding analytics to measure post performance, follower growth, and engagement rates.

- **Improving Content Strategy**: A/B testing different types of posts and adjusting strategies based on audience behavior.

- **Consistency and Content Planning**: Using scheduling tools to maintain a steady flow of high-quality content.

Monetizing Instagram

For those looking to turn Instagram into a source of income, we covered various monetization strategies:

- **Earning Through Sponsored Posts**: Partnering with brands and earning revenue through collaborations.
- **Instagram Affiliate Marketing**: Promoting products and earning commissions.
- **Selling Products and Services**: Using Instagram Shopping and Live Selling to convert followers into customers.

Safety and Account Management

As Instagram continues to grow, ensuring account security and managing interactions effectively is more important than ever. We discussed:

- **Privacy and Security Settings**: Adjusting privacy controls, enabling two-factor authentication, and protecting personal information.
- **Dealing with Negative Comments and Trolls**: Strategies to moderate comments, respond to criticism, and handle online negativity.
- **Managing Multiple Accounts**: Switching between personal and business profiles efficiently and using third-party tools for account management.

Final Thoughts

Instagram is a dynamic platform that continues to evolve, offering new opportunities for personal expression, business growth, and digital marketing. Mastering Instagram requires a mix of creativity, strategic planning, and adaptability.

By implementing the lessons from this book, you can create compelling content, engage with your audience, and grow your presence effectively. Remember, success on Instagram doesn't happen overnight, but with dedication and consistency, you can achieve your goals. Keep experimenting, analyzing, and refining your approach as you continue your Instagram journey.

Now that you've completed this guide, take the next step by applying what you've learned. Stay updated with Instagram's latest features, continue to engage with your audience, and most importantly, enjoy the process!

9.2 Next Steps for Continued Growth

Congratulations on reaching this point in your Instagram journey! By now, you have learned how to set up and optimize your profile, create engaging content, grow your audience, and even explore monetization options. However, Instagram is a constantly evolving platform, and staying ahead requires continuous learning and adaptation. In this chapter, we will explore practical steps to ensure your long-term success and continued growth on Instagram.

1. Stay Updated with Instagram Trends and Features

Instagram frequently introduces new features and updates its algorithm. To remain relevant and competitive, it is crucial to stay informed about these changes. Here's how:

- **Follow Instagram's Official Blog and Social Media**: Instagram often announces updates through its official blog and social media accounts.

- **Join Online Communities and Forums**: Platforms like Reddit, Facebook groups, and Twitter threads can provide insights into emerging trends.

- **Experiment with New Features**: Whenever Instagram releases a new feature (e.g., Reels, Stories, or Shopping), incorporate it into your strategy early.

- **Analyze Competitors and Industry Leaders**: Observe how successful influencers and brands leverage Instagram's latest tools.

2. Refine Your Content Strategy

As your audience grows, your content should evolve to meet their changing needs. Here are a few ways to refine your approach:

- **Use Data-Driven Insights**: Regularly review Instagram Insights to understand what content performs best.

- **Experiment with Different Content Formats**: Mix static posts, videos, carousels, and live sessions to keep your audience engaged.

- **Leverage User-Generated Content (UGC)**: Encourage your followers to create and share content featuring your brand.

- **Develop Thematic Content Series**: Create consistent, ongoing content series that establish a deeper connection with your audience.

3. Strengthen Your Engagement Strategies

Engagement is key to building a loyal community. To keep your audience involved:

- **Respond to Comments and Messages Promptly**: Show your followers that you value their input.

- **Encourage Conversations**: Ask open-ended questions in captions and Instagram Stories.

- **Host Live Q&A Sessions**: Live interactions humanize your brand and build stronger relationships.

- **Run Contests and Giveaways**: Incentivize engagement through interactive campaigns.

- **Collaborate with Other Creators**: Partnering with influencers or brands in your niche can expand your reach.

4. Expand Beyond Instagram

While Instagram is a powerful platform, expanding your presence across other digital channels can help you build a more sustainable brand. Consider the following:

- **Develop a Website or Blog**: Create a space where you can share in-depth content, capture leads, and establish credibility.

- **Grow an Email List**: Use Instagram to drive sign-ups for newsletters, exclusive offers, and updates.

- **Diversify Across Social Media**: Engage on platforms like YouTube, TikTok, Pinterest, and Twitter to reach a broader audience.

- **Repurpose Content**: Turn Instagram posts into blog articles, podcast discussions, or YouTube videos to maximize their lifespan.

5. Monetize and Build a Sustainable Business Model

If you're looking to turn Instagram into a full-time business or side hustle, consider diversifying your revenue streams:

- **Offer Paid Collaborations and Sponsorships**: Work with brands that align with your niche and audience.

- **Launch Your Own Products or Services**: From online courses to e-commerce stores, leverage your Instagram influence.

- **Join Affiliate Marketing Programs**: Earn commissions by promoting relevant products to your followers.

- **Enable Instagram Subscriptions**: Offer exclusive content and perks for a paid audience.

6. Maintain a Growth Mindset

Success on Instagram requires persistence, adaptability, and a willingness to learn. To stay ahead:

- **Invest in Continuous Learning**: Take online courses, read marketing books, and attend industry webinars.

- **Seek Feedback from Your Audience**: Regularly ask your followers what they enjoy and what they'd like to see more of.

- **Analyze Your Competitors**: Observe how other successful creators navigate challenges and implement new strategies.

- **Stay Authentic**: Always prioritize authenticity and genuine connections over shortcuts like buying followers.

Conclusion

Instagram is a dynamic platform that offers endless opportunities for growth. By staying informed, refining your content, engaging effectively, expanding your presence, and diversifying your revenue streams, you can build a sustainable and influential brand. Keep learning, stay adaptable, and enjoy the journey as you continue growing your presence on Instagram!

9.3 Final Thoughts and Encouragement

Congratulations! You have reached the final chapter of this comprehensive guide to Instagram. By now, you should have a solid understanding of how to use Instagram effectively, from setting up your profile to growing your audience, engaging with content, monetizing your presence, and ensuring your security. However, mastering Instagram is not just about knowing the tools and strategies; it is also about cultivating the right mindset and consistently refining your approach.

Embracing the Journey

Instagram, like any other platform, is constantly evolving. New features emerge, algorithms change, and trends shift. The key to long-term success is adaptability. Whether you are using Instagram for personal expression, brand building, or business growth, your journey will be filled with learning experiences. Some posts will perform better than others, some strategies will work while others may not, and there will be moments of both triumph and frustration.

The most successful Instagram users are those who view the platform as a long-term commitment rather than a short-term experiment. Stay curious, experiment with different content formats, and always be willing to adapt.

Staying Motivated

There will be times when you may feel discouraged, especially if your growth is slower than expected. It is important to remember that success on Instagram is not just about numbers—it is about the impact and connections you create. Instead of obsessing over follower counts and engagement rates, focus on providing value to your audience. Here are a few ways to stay motivated:

1. **Celebrate Small Wins** – Every milestone, no matter how small, is a step forward. Whether it is gaining your first 100 followers, receiving meaningful comments, or successfully collaborating with another creator, acknowledge and appreciate your progress.

2. **Engage with Like-Minded People** – Surround yourself with a supportive community. Follow and interact with creators who inspire you, join discussions, and participate in collaborations to keep your enthusiasm high.

3. **Revisit Your Goals** – If you ever feel stuck, take a moment to reflect on why you started. Reevaluate your goals and adjust your strategy as needed. If your original goal was to promote your business but you now find more joy in sharing educational content, embrace the shift.

4. **Take Breaks When Needed** – Social media burnout is real. If you ever feel overwhelmed, do not hesitate to take a short break to recharge. Your audience will still be there when you return, and a fresh perspective can often lead to better content ideas.

The Power of Authenticity

One of the most valuable lessons you can take away from this guide is the importance of authenticity. The most successful accounts on Instagram are not necessarily those with the highest production quality or the most polished posts—they are the ones that connect with their audience in a genuine way. Be yourself. Share your unique perspective, experiences, and passions. People are drawn to authenticity, and your personal touch is what will set you apart in a sea of content creators.

Looking Ahead

As you move forward in your Instagram journey, here are some final tips to keep in mind:

- **Continue Learning** – Stay updated with Instagram's latest features and trends by following official Instagram blogs, social media experts, and relevant online communities.

- **Experiment and Innovate** – Do not be afraid to try new content formats, storytelling techniques, or engagement strategies. Growth often comes from stepping outside your comfort zone.

- **Stay Consistent** – While it is important to adapt, consistency is key. Maintain a steady posting schedule and interact with your audience regularly.

- **Measure Your Progress** – Use Instagram Insights to track your performance and refine your strategy based on what works best.

- **Enjoy the Process** – Instagram should be fun and fulfilling. Focus on creativity, connection, and making a positive impact.

A Final Word of Encouragement

No matter where you are in your Instagram journey, remember that every successful creator, influencer, and business started where you are now—with a single post, a small audience, and a vision. Growth takes time, but with persistence, creativity, and a strategic approach, you will see results.

Use this guide as a foundation, but do not be afraid to carve your own path. Instagram is a platform full of endless possibilities, and the next big success story could be yours.

Now, go forth and create, connect, and conquer the world of Instagram!

Acknowledgment

Dear Reader,

*Thank you for choosing **The Ultimate Instagram Guide: From Beginner to Pro**. I truly appreciate your time and trust in this book as a resource to enhance your Instagram journey. Whether you're just starting out or looking to refine your skills, I hope this guide provides you with valuable insights, practical strategies, and inspiration to make the most of your experience on the platform.*

Your support means the world to me. Writing this book was a labor of love, and knowing that it can help you grow, connect, and succeed on Instagram makes it all worthwhile. If you found this guide helpful, I would love to hear your thoughts! Your feedback, reviews, and shared experiences help improve future editions and reach more readers like you.

Once again, thank you for being a part of this journey. Wishing you success, creativity, and endless possibilities on Instagram!

Best regards,

www.ingramcontent.com/pod-product-compliance
Lightning Source LLC
LaVergne TN
LVHW081334050326
832903LV00024B/1158